ENORMOUS TALONS

ENORMOUS TALONS

The Wild Kingdom's Weapons

RAYAN MUSK

Mohammed Altaf Hussain

Contents

Table of Content

Chapter 1

Introduction to Claws

In the huge embroidery of the regular world, paws arise as quintessential devices of endurance, encapsulating the embodiment of transformative ability across a bunch of animal varieties. These amazing designs, frequently connected with the set of all animals, reach out a long ways past simple instruments for predation; they are diverse transformations that have empowered animals to explore their surroundings, secure food, protect against dangers, and take part in unpredictable social collaborations. From the treetops to the sea profundities, hooks have advanced as adaptable limbs, finely tuned by the powers of regular choice north of millions of years.

At their center, paws are particular designs got from adjusted appendages, regularly the digits, that have gone through extraordinary changes to fill unmistakable needs. The variety of hooks across species mirrors the shifted environmental specialties and ways of life that organic entities possess. Whether it's the considerable claws of flying predators, the retractable paws of large felines, or the strong pliers of scavangers, every transformation addresses the one of a kind difficulties and valuable open doors introduced by various environments.

One of the most notable instances of hooks in the set of all animals can be found among flying predators, especially raptors. These avian hunters, including birds, falcons, and hawks, brag claws that are wonders of accuracy and lethality. Adjusted for catching and immobilizing prey, raptor claws are portrayed by their bended, extremely sharp tips and strong grasp. Birds, for example, utilize their imposing claws to grab fish from waterways or to protect little warm blooded animals with amazing precision, displaying the personal association among structure and capability in the transformative weapons contest.

Wandering into the earthly domain, the catlike family displays a wonderful variety of hooks, each custom-made to the extraordinary requirements of its proprietor. Lions and tigers, among other large felines, have retractable paws that typify flexibility. These retractable paws, equipped for expanding and withdrawing on a case by case basis, empower cats to keep up with the sharpness expected for hunting while at the same time limiting wear during non-savage exercises. Such versatile components add to their ability as trackers as well as highlight the significance of energy preservation in the requesting environments they possess.

In the marine climate, paws take on an alternate structure and capability. Shellfish, like crabs and lobsters, employ strong pliers that act as devices for both predation and guard. These scavanger hooks, frequently uneven, are finely tuned for a scope of exercises, from catching prey and tying down mates to uncovering tunnels. The variety of shapes and sizes in marine hooks features the unpredictable exchange between environmental requests and developmental advancement, with every variation improving the creature's possibilities of endurance in the amphibian world.

Past the domain of predation, hooks additionally assume essential parts in friendly collaborations and regional protection. The intricate romance showcases of birds, highlighting perplexing developments of their paws, act as a demonstration of the double capability of these designs in both endurance and multiplication. Intraspecies battle, frequently saw among different vertebrates, includes the sending of hooks as considerable weapons in disagreements about assets or mates. The flexibility of paws for both hostile and guarded purposes highlights their importance in the mind boggling elements of natural cooperations.

Additionally, hooks have tracked down utility in motion, permitting specific species to cross testing scenes with unmatched readiness. Arboreal animals, for example, primates and a few reptiles, influence their paws to grasp onto branches and explore the mind boggling overhang of the woods. These transformations empower them to get to assets that would be generally unreachable, displaying the developmental benefits presented by these flexible limbs.

The universe of paws is a spellbinding investigation into the complexities of transformative science and natural variety.

These transformations, sharpened by the tenacious powers of normal choice, offer a brief look into the heap manners by which life has formed itself to flourish in different territories. Whether in the air, ashore, or underneath the waves, paws stand as demonstrations of the creativity of nature, showing that structure and capability are unpredictably laced in the never-ending dance of endurance.

1.1: The Evolutionary Significance

The developmental meaning of paws rises above simple physical variations; it is a demonstration of the unique transaction among life forms and their surroundings over topographical ages. As essential parts of different species' tool compartments, paws address the perfection of developmental cycles that have profoundly influenced life's capacity to explore, interface, and get by. Understanding the transformative meaning of paws requires digging into the many-sided trap of regular determination, environmental tensions, and versatile reactions that have shaped these designs into multifunctional ponders.

In the developmental theater, the rise of hooks implies a significant reaction to the specific tensions forced by the climate. The advancement of these specific designs mirrors nature's tenacious quest for effectiveness, permitting living beings to take advantage of assets and adapt to difficulties in their biological specialties. The developmental weapons contest, portrayed by the ceaseless battle for endurance, has prompted the refinement and enhancement of paws as versatile answers for explicit ecological requests.

At its center, the advancement of paws is profoundly interwoven with the mission for food. Ruthless species, specifically, have outfit the capability of hooks as deadly weapons for catching and quelling prey. Raptors, exemplified by birds and falcons, feature a stunning variation of paws custom-made for flying hunting. The bended and dangerously sharp claws of these flying predators are accuracy instruments, finely tuned to get a handle on and immobilize prey with unrivaled exactness. The transformative benefit gave by such variations is obvious in the progress of these hunters, as they exploit the skies to get their place on the pecking order.

The earthly scene offers a different exhibit of hook transformations, with large felines standing apart as models of developmental resourcefulness. The retractable hooks of lions, tigers, and other cat hunters epitomize a fragile harmony among hostile and guarded functionalities. Retractable hooks, a transformative development, permit these carnivores to keep up with sharpness for hunting while at the same time limiting wear during non-ruthless exercises. This double reason transformation upgrades the proficiency of large felines in exploring the difficulties of their biological systems, underlining the job of paws as weapons as well as devices for energy preservation.

Shellfish, abiding in the amphibian domains, grandstand one more feature of the developmental meaning of hooks. From crabs to lobsters, these marine arthropods use strong pliers that have developed for a huge number of purposes. The imbalance of scavanger hooks frequently reflects specific capabilities, for example, catching prey, getting mates, or exhuming tunnels. The flexibility of these designs highlights the versatility of paws in answering the novel requests of marine conditions. Through endless ages of refinement, marine scavangers have manufactured a different exhibit of paw transformations that work with their endurance and propagation in the powerful maritime environments.

Past the domain of predation, paws assume vital parts in friendly elements and regional connections. Avian romance showcases, including mind boggling developments of hooks, act as enrapturing instances of how these designs add to regenerative achievement. The developmental dance of romance, molded by the language of paws, features the job of these transformations in mate determination and the propagation of hereditary characteristics. Intra-species battle, saw in different well evolved creatures, frequently includes the arrangement of hooks as imposing weapons in disagreements about assets or mates. The transformative meaning of hooks in these situations lies in their double job as instruments of both rivalry and collaboration inside an animal groups.

Besides, the train benefits gave by paws play had a vital impact in the transformative progress of certain taxa. Arboreal animals, going from primates to reptiles, have advanced hooks adjusted for holding onto branches and exploring the intricate covering of backwoods. This transformation upgrades their dexterity, permitting them to get to assets and dodge hunters in the complicated three-layered scenes they possess. The developmental meaning of paws in headway mirrors the particular tensions forced by unambiguous territories, outlining how these designs add to the general wellness of species in their separate surroundings.

The unpredictable embroidered artwork of development is woven with the strings of variation and endurance, and hooks stand as many-sided strings in this great account. The different signs of hooks across species highlight the flexibility of these designs as answers for the horde challenges presented by the regular world. Every variation, whether in the air, ashore, or in the water, is a demonstration of the tireless imagination of life in its quest for presence.

The transformative meaning of hooks is a rich and complex story that ranges across taxa and biological systems. From the deadly accuracy of raptor claws to the multifunctional flexibility of shellfish pliers, hooks epitomize the developmental arrangements created by endless ages in light of the ceaseless requests of endurance. The narrative of paws isn't simply a story of physical highlights; it is an account of the interminable dance among creatures and their surroundings, representing how the powers of normal choice have profoundly influenced life into a bunch of structures, each adjusted for the special difficulties and valuable open doors introduced by the consistently impacting world.

1.2: Functionality in the Animal Kingdom

The usefulness of hooks inside the collective of animals rises above simple physical variations; it is a demonstration of the powerful transaction among structure and capability that has developed north of millions of years. Paws, as flexible designs, have been sharpened by the powers of regular choice to fill a large number of needs across different species, mirroring the versatile resourcefulness of life in different natural specialties. From predation and guard to social cooperations and natural route, the usefulness of paws is an enamoring investigation into the nuanced manners by which life forms have developed to address the difficulties of their individual living spaces.

At its most basic level, the usefulness of hooks is exemplified in the domain of predation. Among flying predators, the advancement of hooks into imposing claws addresses a dazzling variation for catching and immobilizing prey. Birds, falcons, and hawks, with their bended and extremely sharp claws, take part in flying hunting with unmatched accuracy. These specific designs are not simply instruments for getting food; they are finely tuned weapons that epitomize the convergence of developmental proficiency and ruthless ability. The usefulness of raptor claws stretches out past the demonstration of hunting to the actual pith of endurance, delineating how paws have become inseparable from the basic dance of hunter and prey.

In the earthly scene, large felines embody one more feature of the usefulness of hooks. Lions, tigers, and other cat hunters use retractable paws that act as multifunctional apparatuses for exploring their surroundings. The flexibility of retractable paws is a demonstration of their double job in hostile and protective situations. During hunting, these paws broaden, giving the fundamental sharpness to catching and stifling prey. In non-ruthless exercises, the capacity to withdraw paws limits wear, featuring the energy-saving part of their usefulness. This adaptability highlights how paws, as transformative developments, have been shaped to fulfill the different needs of endurance in the complicated environments occupied by enormous felines.

Shellfish abiding in marine conditions offer one more point of view on the usefulness of hooks. From crabs to lobsters, these arthropods employ strong pliers that fill a horde of needs. The imbalance frequently saw in scavanger hooks reflects specialization for undertakings, for example, catching prey, getting mates, or uncovering tunnels. The usefulness of scavanger paws reaches out past predation, exhibiting their flexibility in answering a scope of natural difficulties. In the complexities of submerged life, these designs are not simply weapons; they are diverse devices that empower shellfish to explore the perplexing elements of marine biological systems.

The usefulness of hooks, in any case, reaches out past the prompt demonstration of acquiring food. Social collaborations and regional guard are fields where hooks assume significant parts.

Avian romance presentations, frequently including perplexing developments of hooks, epitomize how these designs add to conceptive achievement. The usefulness of paws in romance isn't exclusively about animosity or rivalry however is complicatedly woven into the language of mate determination and species propagation. Essentially, intra-species battle among warm blooded creatures, set apart by the organization of paws, features the double job of these designs as instruments of both rivalry and participation inside an animal groups. The usefulness of hooks in friendly elements highlights their importance in forming the complicated connections that characterize life inside a given biological system.

Besides, the usefulness of hooks reaches out to motion, offering specific species a critical benefit in exploring their surroundings. Arboreal animals, going from primates to reptiles, use their hooks for holding onto branches and crossing the complicated shade of backwoods. The usefulness of hooks in velocity is a demonstration of their flexibility, permitting species to get to assets and sidestep hunters in three-layered scenes. The transformative meaning of hooks in movement stresses their job in procuring food as well as in the general wellness of an animal types inside its natural specialty.

The mind boggling embroidery of usefulness woven by hooks across various species highlights the adaptability of these designs as devices of endurance. From the deadly accuracy of raptor claws to the multifunctional adaptability of scavanger pliers, hooks epitomize the different methodologies that life has created to flourish in shifted natural surroundings. The usefulness of hooks is certainly not a static quality; rather, it is a unique impression of the continuous discourse among organic entities and their surroundings, formed by the constant powers of regular determination.

The usefulness of paws inside the animals of the world collectively is a nuanced investigation into the horde manners by which life has adjusted to its environmental factors. From the base demonstration of predation to the complexities of social elements and ecological route, paws act as vital devices that have advanced to address the diverse difficulties of endurance. The tale of usefulness in the animals of the world collectively is a demonstration of the many-sided dance of transformation, a story where the structure and capability of hooks entwine to make a rich embroidery of life in its unending quest for presence.

1.3: Notable Examples in Nature

In the complex mosaic of the normal world, hooks stand as model transformations, and their different appearances across species act as remarkable instances of developmental creativity. From the skies to the profundities of the sea, nature has shaped a variety of paws, each finely tuned to address the particular difficulties introduced by various conditions. These eminent models feature the wonderful variety of life as well as highlight the flexibility and usefulness of paws as urgent parts of step by step processes for surviving.

One of the most notorious instances of hooks in the regular world can be found among flying predators, especially birds. The great range of a falcon's wings, combined with its impressive claws, represents the encapsulation of elevated hunting. The size, shape, and ebb and flow of these claws are finely tuned for accuracy and lethality. At the point when a falcon slips upon its prey, its claws reach out with careful accuracy, locking onto the objective with a bad habit like grasp. This astounding transformation permits hawks to be capable trackers, getting their place at the summit of the well established pecking order in different biological systems.

Likewise, birds of prey and hawks, direct relations of falcons, additionally show remarkable instances of hooks adjusted for airborne ability. The peregrine bird of prey, specifically, is famous for its surprising pace during plunges, an accomplishment made conceivable by its smoothed out body and extremely sharp claws. As it rushes towards its prey, the peregrine hawk sends its paws with unmatched precision, exhibiting the developmental artfulness of these designs. These avian hunters, with their eminent instances of hooks, epitomize the cooperative energy among structure and capability in the persistent quest for endurance.

On the earthbound front, huge felines give one more convincing representation of essential paws in nature. Lions, tigers, cheetahs, and panthers — all individuals from the felid family — have retractable hooks that highlight their flexibility and adaptability. The retractable idea of these paws permits huge felines to keep up with their sharpness for hunting while at the same time limiting wear during different exercises. Cheetahs, known for their momentous speed, use their paws for catching prey as well as for building up momentum during rapid pursuits. These prominent models in the felid family feature the transformative meaning of paws as devices finely tuned for both predation and ecological collaboration.

Wandering into the marine domain, shellfish contribute one more captivating aspect to the collection of remarkable hooks in nature. Crabs, with their unmistakable pliers, grandstand a wide assortment of variations custom-made for different capabilities. The coconut crab, for example, brags strong paws skilled airing out coconuts, showing the flexibility of these designs past predation. The fiddler crab, with its deviated paws, takes part in intricate romance presentations, using its curiously large hook as a visual and acoustic sign to draw in mates. The loner crab, albeit not having its own paws, utilizes shells for security — a novel transformation in the more extensive setting of hook usefulness in the marine climate.

Besides, the maritime domain acquaints us with the mantis shrimp, a marine shellfish praised for its momentous dactyl clubs. These particular appendages, looking like boxing gloves, are equipped for conveying strong blows at unimaginable velocities. The mantis shrimp utilizes its impressive paws for hunting, tearing open the shells of prey with shocking power. The intricacy of the mantis shrimp's paws, furnished with particular elements for various undertakings, fills in as an essential illustration of the complexities that can emerge in the development of these designs in marine conditions.

In the arboreal world, the variations of primates give extra instances of imperative hooks. Lemurs, for example, have prepping paws — particular transformations that guide in the fastidious cleaning of fur. These preparing hooks, portrayed by their shape and size, permit lemurs to keep up with cleanliness and social bonds inside their gatherings. The usefulness of these paws stretches out past predation, featuring the nuanced jobs hooks can play in the social ways of behaving of species possessing explicit environmental specialties.

The variety of eminent paws isn't restricted to explicit environments; it reaches out to the bug world, where variations have developed for a horde of capabilities. The imploring mantis, known for its savage ability, flaunts spiked forelimbs that look like considerable paws. These specific designs are adroit at catching and immobilizing prey, displaying the transformative weapons contest among hunters and their possible casualties. Additionally, subterranean insects, with their mandibles working as considerable hooks, display outstanding instances of variations for errands going from guard to scavenging.

The developmental meaning of outstanding hooks is additionally underlined while thinking about the biological interaction between species. For instance, the communication among hunter and prey frequently results in a coevolutionary dance, where variations and counter-transformations shape the direction of the two species. The hooks of hunters, sharpened by the requests of hunting, drive the advancement of guarded methodologies in prey species. This many-sided dance of variation and counter-transformation highlights the powerful idea of biological systems, where outstanding hooks act as impetuses for developmental change.

Growing our investigation of eminent paws in nature, we dig into the domain of 8-legged creature, where bugs show a striking variety of transformations. Bug silk, frequently alluded to as their "outer paws," serves a critical job in predation, cover development, and conceptive systems. The silk-turning organs, known as spinnerets, empower bugs to deliver an assortment of silk types, each custom-made to explicit capabilities. The sphere winding around bug, for example, conveys silk to develop unpredictable networks for entrapping prey. The outstanding illustration of arachnid silk highlights how hooks, for this situation, stretch out past actual designs to incorporate silk-creating variations that improve endurance in the 8-legged creature world.

Critical instances of paws additionally arise in the avian domain past flying predators. Larks, with their different snout shapes, feature transformations that capability as particular hooks. The crossbill, portrayed by its exceptional crossed mouth, represents a prominent variation for removing seeds from conifer cones. This bill, suggestive of a couple of interlocking pincers, permits the crossbill to get into cone scales and access the nutritious seeds inside. The usefulness of the crossbill's mouth fills in as a demonstration of the different manners by which variations similar to paws can appear in changed avian genealogies.

With regards to reptiles, the notorious illustration of hooks is frequently connected with the powerful Komodo mythical beast. While their essential hunting procedure includes strong jaws and toxin, the Komodo mythical serpent's hooks assume a huge part in repressing prey and working with development. The sharp, bended paws of these enormous reptiles epitomize transformations for grasping and tearing, adding to their prosperity as dominant hunters in their local living spaces. The usefulness of Komodo winged serpent paws is a distinct update that transformations inside the reptilian world stretch out past teeth and jaws to incorporate specific appendages that upgrade ruthless proficiency.

Past the set of all animals, the plant world offers a charming point of view on the idea of paws. Certain plants, for example, the pitcher plant, have adjusted leaves that go about as entanglement traps. The edge of these pitcher-molded leaves capabilities similar to hooks, drawing bugs into the snare where they become caught and hence processed by the plant. The variation of pitcher plants features how concurrent development can prompt the improvement of designs comparable to paws, though in a herbal setting.

A captivating illustration of hooks in the marine climate is seen in the mantis shrimp. With strong, hammer-like limbs, the mantis shrimp's hooks are fit for conveying annihilating blows at staggering velocities. These particular appendages serve various capabilities, including hunting, safeguard, and correspondence. The mantis shrimp's capacity to air out hard-shelled prey with its impressive hooks features the flexibility of these designs in marine environments. The transformative weapons contest between the mantis shrimp and its prey grandstands the way in which prominent hooks are unpredictably entwined with the elements of predation and variation in the maritime domain.

In the domain of bugs, the mantis shows forelimbs that look like spiked hooks, adjusted for catching and immobilizing prey. The imploring mantis exhibits a wonderful union with the ruthless variations seen in bigger hunters, like huge felines and raptors. The getting a handle on usefulness of mantis forelimbs highlights how paws, in different structures, have developed freely across different taxa, combining on comparable answers for endurance in their separate surroundings.

Moreover, the variation of paws for ecological route is exemplified in the fascinating instance of the yes, a nighttime lemur from Madagascar. The yes has a long, slim finger with a particular hook like nail, utilized for tapping on tree husk to find stowed away bug hatchlings. This extraordinary variation permits the yes to utilize a type of echolocation, tuning in for the sounds delivered by wood-exhausting bugs inside tree trunks. The particular paw like nail of the yes' stretched finger fills in as an uncommon illustration of how hooks can advance for errands past predation, exhibiting the adaptability of these designs in the mind boggling universe of natural connections.

The far reaching study of prominent paws across assorted taxa underlines their versatile importance in the persistent battle for endurance. The useful variety saw in paws, from predation and safeguard to social associations and natural route, highlights their significant job in molding the developmental directions of endless species. Remarkable hooks are not just natural devices for endurance; they are images of the multifaceted connections among creatures and their surroundings, delineating how structure and capability join in the stupendous woven artwork of life.

The investigation of prominent paws in nature uncovers an enamoring story of transformative development and versatility. From the skies to the sea profundities, and from the minute universe of bugs to the transcending trees of the rainforest, paws have developed in heap frames, each finely tuned to address the exceptional difficulties introduced by assorted environments. The narratives of remarkable paws go past the simple assessment of physical designs; they epitomize the pith of life's interminable hit the dance floor with its environmental elements. As we keep on disentangling the secrets of the regular world, prominent paws act as signs, directing us through the interesting excursion of transformation, endurance, and the constant quest for presence.

1.4: Human Fascination and Fear

The interest and dread evoked by hooks, particularly while thinking about their signs in the animals of the world collectively, are well established in the human mind. Since days of yore, people have been spellbound by the impressive and frequently grand nature of hooks in different animals. This double reaction, mixing interest and dread, addresses the mind boggling connection among humankind and the untamed parts of the regular world.

At the core of human interest with hooks lies a base association with our own endurance impulses. In the earliest phases of human advancement, our precursors wrestled with similar difficulties looked by different species — predation, rivalry for assets, and the consistent battle for endurance. The considerable paws of dominant hunters, like huge felines and flying predators, became emblematic portrayals of both power and risk. People, as they continued looking for predominance over the regular world, were normally attracted to these notorious images of solidarity, versatility, and savage ability.

Antiquities from old civic establishments, going from cave works of art to unpredictable carvings, take the stand concerning mankind's interest with hooks. These portrayals frequently depict creatures with misrepresented paws, accentuating their importance in the aggregate human cognizance. The emblematic significance of paws reaches out past simple utilitarian transformations; it digs into the domains of folklore, legends, and social imagery, where hooks frequently address base powers, both innovative and damaging.

In antiquated societies, paws were oftentimes connected with gods and legendary animals. The Egyptian goddess Sekhmet, portrayed with lioness paws, epitomized both the defensive and horrendous parts of heavenly power. In Norse folklore, the legendary wolf Fenrir was described by fearsome paws, representing confusion and looming destruction. These social portrayals highlight the well established interest and adoration people have held for hooks from the beginning of time, frequently crediting them with extraordinary characteristics and heavenly importance.

Past folklore, the creature motivated themes of paws have saturated different parts of human workmanship and plan. From antiquated to contemporary times, paws have enhanced adornments, weaponry, and heraldic images, filling in as strong seals of solidarity, mental fortitude, and savagery. The archaic act of integrating creature paws into the plan of knight's covering, for example, represents the entwining of human interest with hooks and the journey for emblematic strength despite misfortune.

In any case, close by interest, there exists a characteristic trepidation related with hooks. This dread is established in the base acknowledgment of paws as powerful instruments of predation and risk. People, as prey creatures themselves in the beginning phases of advancement, fostered a natural reaction to seeing sharp, pointed paws. The feeling of dread toward hooks is profoundly implanted in the endurance components of the human cerebrum, filling in as an instinctive sign of the wild and eccentric nature of the normal world.

The apprehension about hooks isn't restricted to the domain of the untamed wild. It pervades different parts of human culture, forming stories in writing, legends, and famous media. The model of the colossal animal with dangerously sharp paws includes conspicuously in legendary stories and fantasies, appearing as winged serpents, witches, or legendary monsters. These accounts tap into the base apprehension implanted in the human mind, depicting paws as instruments of vindictiveness and approaching risk.

In the realm of film and writing, the feeling of dread toward hooks finds articulation in notable characters, for example, werewolves and vampires, whose paws represent the colossal and extraordinary. The instinctive effect of these imaginary animals, with their fearsome hooks, resounds with crowds, profiting by the inborn human anxiety toward the obscure and the untamed. The depiction of paws as devices of ghastliness and animosity supports the firmly established misgiving that waits in the aggregate human creative mind.

Besides, the apprehension about hooks isn't exclusively restricted to the domain of imagination. Genuine experiences with creatures having impressive hooks can set off a basic trepidation reaction, even in present day, urbanized social orders.

Natural life narratives and close experiences with dominant hunters frequently inspire a blend of stunningness and fear, as the crude force of hooks becomes discernible. Notwithstanding the social and mechanical headways that recognize contemporary human social orders, the instinctual dread of hooks remains engraved in our shared awareness.

Strangely, the interest and feeling of dread toward paws are not fundamentally unrelated; rather, they exist together in a sensitive equilibrium inside the human mind. This double reaction can be seen in different social practices, where customs and images related with paws act as both defensive charms and strong articulations of force. Talismans and charms highlighting paw themes are frequently worn as images of solidarity and flexibility, saddling the sensational characteristics of hooks to avoid apparent dangers.

The division of interest and dread encompassing hooks likewise reaches out to the domain of sporting exercises. People, attracted to the excitement of experiencing risky natural life, frequently look for controlled conditions, like zoos and natural life asylums, to observe the magnificence of animals with considerable paws. This controlled openness permits people to draw in with their basic interest while moderating the innate apprehension related with untamed nature. Besides, exercises, for example, bird-watching and untamed life photography give roads to people to see the value in the excellence of paws in a harmless setting.

In a more emblematic sense, the mix of hook symbolism in mainstream society fills in for of standing up to and investigating human feelings of dread. Repulsiveness classifications in writing and film influence the feeling of dread toward hooks as a story device, offering crowds a soothing involvement with a controlled climate. The made up investigation of paws as instruments of peril permits people to wrestle with base feelings of dread while securely tucked away inside the domain of fiction.

The oddity of interest and dread related with paws reflects humankind's intricate relationship with the regular world. As present day cultures keep on reducing most, if not all, connection with the wild, the division continues as an indication of the basic powers that formed human development. Paws, as images of both excellence and risk, act as an extension between the disinfected scenes of metropolitan living and the untamed wild that once characterized the human experience.

Growing our investigation of the human interest and apprehension about hooks, it's fundamental to dive into the physiological and mental aspects that underlie these intricate feelings. The sensational and fearsome characteristics of hooks trigger significant responses inside the human brain and body, offering experiences into the perplexing manners by which our developmental legacy keeps on forming our discernments and reactions.

Physiologically, the feeling of dread toward hooks is profoundly imbued in the human pressure reaction framework. When defied with boosts related with hooks — whether genuine or emblematic — the amygdala, a piece of the mind liable for handling feelings, especially dread, is initiated. This triggers a fountain of physiological responses, including the arrival of stress chemicals like cortisol and adrenaline. The uplifted condition of readiness, expanded pulse, and fast breathing are versatile reactions that have developed over centuries to set up the body for an expected danger.

With regards to hooks, the physiological trepidation reaction is a demonstration of their verifiable importance as signs of risk in the regular habitat. In hereditary scenes, where experiences with hunters were continuous, people who fostered an elevated aversion to signals related with hooks were bound to get by and pass on their qualities. Subsequently, the apprehension about paws turned out to be profoundly implanted in the human hereditary code, molding the manner in which we see and respond to these imposing designs.

On the other hand, the interest with paws likewise sets off a physiological reaction, though one portrayed by a feeling of stunningness and marvel. The enactment of remuneration focuses in the cerebrum, including the arrival of synapses like dopamine, goes with the experience of interest. This uplifting feedback fills in as a component that supports exploratory way of behaving and learning. With regards to hooks, the interest might come from an enthusiasm for their useful variations, tasteful magnificence, or the emblematic power they exemplify.

The concurrence of dread and interest in the human reaction to hooks is a demonstration of the unpredictable transaction between our transformative past and our contemporary mental cycles. The duality of these feelings mirrors the incomprehensible idea of our relationship with the wild — a perplexing dance among fascination and aversion, veneration and fear.

Mentally, the human interest with paws frequently reaches out past their nearby genuineness to emblematic portrayals. Paws, as images of force and strength, become illustrations for basic impulses and untamed powers. This emblematic reverberation is obvious in different social articulations, where hooks are utilized to convey traits like fortitude, versatility, and steadiness.

The prime example of the legend with hooks, tracked down in fantasies and legends across societies, epitomizes the mental allure of these images. Whether as the Greek legend Heracles, whose incredible twelve works included confronting the Nemean lion with its impervious paws, or the Wonder Comics character Wolverine, with retractable hooks and regenerative powers, the paradigm of the mauled legend reverberates with crowds on a profound mental level. It takes advantage of the aggregate human mind, where the imagery of hooks turns into a story device for investigating topics of win over difficulty and the unyielding soul.

Alternately, the mental anxiety toward hooks frequently appears in social stories that portray paws as instruments of perniciousness. Beasts, evil presences, and legendary monsters with dangerously sharp paws become encapsulations of fear, taking advantage of the basic openings of the human creative mind. The mental trepidation related with these portrayals fills in as a preventative component, helping people to remember the potential perils innate in the untamed parts of the normal world.

In the advanced time, where the promptness of actual dangers from wild creatures has decreased, the mental feeling of dread toward paws has taken on new aspects. Blood and gore films and spine chillers frequently exploit the feeling of dread toward paws as an instinctive and reminiscent component. Animals with sharp paws, whether earthbound or extraterrestrial, keep on being focal figures with sickening dread stories, playing on the firmly established fears engraved in the human mind through centuries of development.

In addition, the anxiety toward hooks is in some cases uplifted by the component of capriciousness related with wild creatures. In controlled conditions, for example, zoos or untamed life holds, experiences with huge hunters can bring out a blend of wonderment and fear. Indeed, even behind the security of glass obstructions, the base apprehension reaction can be set off when stood up to with the crude power and sharp hooks of dominant hunters. This mental response highlights the persevering through effect of developmental cycles on human insight, where the apprehension about paws remains profoundly implanted notwithstanding the facade of innovation.

In the domain of mainstream society, where paws are regularly utilized as visual themes, the mental effect reaches out past prompt close to home reactions. The symbolism of paws frequently fills in as a social shorthand, summoning a scope of affiliations attached to strength, risk, and unusualness. Promoting, marking, and media enterprises influence the mental reverberation of hooks to pass on messages going from the savagery of sports groups to the power of shopper items. The intrinsic mental responses to paws become apparatuses for molding discernments and getting explicit profound reactions in crowds.

The double idea of human reactions to paws — at the same time intriguing and dread actuating — has suggestions for different parts of our lives, from diversion and craftsmanship to promoting and marking. It mirrors a sensitive harmony between our firmly established impulses and the mental cycles that shape our contemporary insights. This transaction between the base and the mental adds to the getting through allure and strength of paws as images in the human mind.

In a more extensive social setting, the interest and anxiety toward paws are likewise reflected in cultural perspectives toward untamed life protection and natural stewardship. As human exercises progressively infringe upon regular natural surroundings, the apprehension about paws can be weaponized to advocate for the insurance of biological systems and the species that occupy them.

The representative force of paws, whether employed by hunters or utilized for emblematic purposes, turns into a mobilizing point for natural missions, encouraging people to face their feelings of dread and draw in with the basic of protection.

Instructive drives and nature narratives, while underlining the excellence and significance of biodiversity, frequently influence the feeling of dread toward hooks for of drawing in crowds. The juxtaposition of spectacular film with hunters exhibiting their imposing hooks makes a convincing story that rises above simple narrative composition. It turns into an instinctive and genuinely charged insight, reverberating with crowds on a base level and encouraging a more profound association with the normal world.

The human interest and anxiety toward paws are profoundly interlaced with our developmental legacy, forming both our physiological and mental reactions. The concurrence of these feelings mirrors the multifaceted connection among people and the untamed parts of the regular world. Whether as images of force and strength or as instruments of dread and risk, hooks proceed to spellbind and disrupt the human creative mind. The persevering through effect of these complicated feelings is apparent in social articulations, creative portrayals, and cultural perspectives toward nature. As we explore the intricacies of the cutting edge world, the double reactions to paws act as a wake up call of the getting through tradition of our transformative past and the complicated exchange among sense and discernment in molding human insights.

Chapter 2

Giants of the Clawed Realm

The monsters of the ripped at domain, gigantic and considerable animals enriched with strong paws, stand as great models of transformative variation and biological predominance. In different biological systems across the globe, these monsters have cut out specialties as dominant hunters, utilizing their imposing hooks for predation as well as apparatuses for endurance and guard. From the notable wild bear of North America to the perplexing monster insect eating animal of South America, the pawed goliaths exhibit the different manners by which hooks have advanced to shape the environmental scenes they occupy.

In the rough wild of North America, the mountain bear (Ursus arctos horribilis) remains as an image of both wonder and fear. With strong appendages and long, bended paws, grizzlies are very much adjusted to their considerable job as dominant hunters. The usefulness of grizzly paws reaches out past predation; these enormous members are additionally utilized for digging, unearthing roots, tubers, and tunneling creatures. In the occasional quest for food, mountain bears utilize their paws to rummage for nutritious vegetation, adding to their capacity to flourish in various environments, from thick timberlands to snow capped knolls.

The paws of mountain bears, which can surpass four creeps long, are imposing weapons as well as fundamental devices for exploring the difficulties of their surroundings. During the yearly salmon runs, grizzlies grandstand their fishing ability by deftly swiping at relocating fish in quick, unequivocal developments. The bended paws, intended for getting a handle on and getting prey, become accuracy instruments in the complex dance among hunter and prey. The developmental meaning of grizzly paws lies in their job as weapons as well as in their flexibility as apparatuses that upgrade the bear's versatility in different biological systems.

Venturing out to the huge meadows of South America, the monster insect eating animal (Myrmecophaga tridactyla) arises as a mysterious goliath of the mauled domain. In spite of being apparently subtle, the goliath insect eating animal has novel variations that make it a particular hunter. The most prominent of these transformations are its stretched forelimbs and imposing paws. The goliath insect eating animal's hooks are bended and well honed, arriving at lengths of up to four inches. While the monster insect eating animal needs teeth, its strong hooks act as compelling instruments for tearing open termite hills and subterranean insect homes — an essential food source.

The usefulness of the monster insect eating animal's paws is a wonderful illustration of concurrent advancement, where unmistakable species freely foster comparative transformations. For this situation, the goliath insect eating animal's hooks look similar to those of the more well known hunters. The noteworthy length and sharpness of these hooks empower the monster insect eating animal to easily destroy bug homes, getting to the nutritious occupants inside. The transformative importance lies in the productivity and specialization of these paws, permitting the goliath insect eating animal to flourish in its remarkable natural specialty.

Directing our concentration toward the different environments of Asia, the blurred panther (Neofelis nebulosa) arises as a magnetic cat monster of the mauled domain. Local to the thick woods of Southeast Asia, the blurred panther has remarkable transformations that put it aside from other large felines. One of the most striking highlights is its imposing hooks, which are bizarrely long with respect to its body size. The blurred panther's paws are sharp and semi-retractable, considering extraordinary climbing skills.

The usefulness of the obfuscated panther's hooks is interlaced with its arboreal way of life. Not at all like other large felines that are fundamentally earthly, the obfuscated panther is adroit at exploring the complicated covering of tropical backwoods. The long hooks give the important grasp to climbing trees, following prey, and looking for shelter from likely hunters. This variation features the job of hooks as devices for predation as well as critical parts of movement in unambiguous natural surroundings. The obfuscated panther's presence as a ripped at goliath in the treetops highlights the variety of cat transformations inside the bigger group of huge felines.

Wandering into the sea-going domains, the coconut crab (Birgus latro) of the Indian and Pacific Seas arises as a mauled monster with an unmistakable way of life. In spite of being regularly alluded to as a crab, the coconut crab is all the more firmly connected with earthbound recluse crabs. What separates this animal is its gigantic size and strong paws. The coconut crab is the biggest earthly arthropod, and its paws, looking like impressive pliers, are vigorous and adjusted for different assignments.

The usefulness of the coconut crab's hooks stretches out past predation to incorporate ways of behaving like climbing and correspondence. With a leg range that can surpass three feet, coconut crabs are capable climbers, utilizing their strong hooks to rise trees and bluffs looking for food and reasonable settling destinations. Furthermore, these paws serve an imperative job in correspondence and contest between people, particularly during the mating season. The transformative importance lies in the multifunctionality of the coconut crab's hooks, permitting it to flourish in both earthly and beach front conditions.

In the huge scope of African savannas, the African lion (Panthera leo) remains as a notorious monster of the pawed domain. Lions, portrayed by their social construction and strong actual properties, have impressive retractable hooks. While not as long as those of bears, the lion's paws are sharp, bended, and impeccably adjusted for holding and severing prey. The usefulness of lion paws is generally clear during chases, where they assume a pivotal part in catching and curbing prey.

The developmental meaning of lion paws lies in their commitment to helpful hunting techniques. Lions, known for their social construction, frequently chase in gatherings, depending on collaboration and composed endeavors to cut down enormous prey. The imposing hooks of lions supplement their strong jaws, making a deadly blend for dispatching prey productively. The retractable idea of the paws permits lions to save them sharp for hunting while at the same time limiting wear during different exercises. With regards to the African savanna, lion hooks address a zenith of developmental variation, finely tuned for the difficulties of helpful hunting in far reaching meadows.

Digging into the marine domain, the mantis shrimp (Stomatopoda) arises as a phenomenal ripped at goliath occupying coral reefs and shallow seaside waters. Mantis shrimp are famous for their specific raptorial limbs, which are profoundly adjusted for catching prey. These extremities, looking like strong hooks, are outfitted with sharp spines and capability as lightning-quick striking components. The usefulness of mantis shrimp paws lies in their extraordinary speed and power, permitting these marine hunters to quell prey with shocking proficiency.

The transformative meaning of mantis shrimp hooks is a demonstration of the weapons contest among hunters and prey in the mind boggling submerged environments.

The mantis shrimp's capacity to hit with staggering velocity and power empowers it to catch quick prey, like fish and scavangers. The flexibility of mantis shrimp hooks, which can be adjusted for various hunting methodologies, grandstands the versatility and intricacy of transformative cycles in marine conditions.

These monsters of the ripped at domain, spreading over different living spaces and taxa, give a window into the diverse universe of developmental transformation. The usefulness of their paws reaches out past simple predation, incorporating a scope of ways of behaving and biological jobs. From the rough territories of North America to the tropical woodlands of Asia and the sea-going domains of the sea, these pawed monsters outline the variety of methodologies that have developed to address the difficulties of endurance.

Additionally, the developmental meaning of these pawed goliaths goes past their nearby environmental jobs; it stretches out to their social and emblematic significance. In different societies, these animals have become images of solidarity, flexibility, and the complex dance among hunter and prey. The presence of impressive hooks in the collective of animals reverberates with human minds, starting both interest and, on occasion, dread.

The investigation of these mauled monsters gives important experiences into the nuanced connections among structure and capability in the regular world. Hooks, as versatile designs, address arrangements created by development to address the particular difficulties presented by different conditions. The multifunctionality of paws, filling in as apparatuses for predation, movement, correspondence, and guard, exhibits the unpredictable manners by which organic entities have calibrated these designs to guarantee their endurance and progress in the amazing woven artwork of life.

Proceeding with our investigation of the monsters of the pawed domain, we shift our concentration to the baffling and subtle wolverine (gulo) of the northern boreal backwoods and uneven locales. Frequently alluded to as the "mountain villain" or "skunk bear," the wolverine has strong appendages and sharp, non-retractable hooks that add to its fearsome standing. Notwithstanding its moderately humble size contrasted with other dominant hunters, the wolverine's paws are impressive apparatuses for endurance in cruel, snow-shrouded scenes.

The usefulness of the wolverine's hooks is especially apparent in their job as proficient digging instruments. Wolverines are known for their rummaging ways of behaving and capacity to find covered bodies underneath the snow. Their sharp paws empower them to uncover through thick snowpack with amazing rate and accuracy. This transformation is pivotal for getting food throughout the cold weather months when prey might be scant, underscoring the flexibility of paws in tending to explicit biological difficulties.

Furthermore, the wolverine's paws are utilized during regional stamping ways of behaving. Wolverines have enormous regions, and people use fragrance stamping and scratching to portray their limits. The hooks assume a part in this checking conduct, leaving noticeable signs on trees and shakes. The mix of strong appendages and sharp hooks permits wolverines to participate in both hostile and cautious connections, displaying the versatile meaning of these designs with regards to their remarkable environmental specialty.

In the extensive meadows of South America, the monster armadillo (Priodontes maximus) arises as a pawed goliath with an unmistakable covering plated outside. Regardless of its impressive appearance, the monster armadillo is principally a digger, depending on its strong forelimbs and enormous, vigorous paws to uncover tunnels for sanctuary and searching. The paws of the goliath armadillo are adjusted for diving into hard soils, permitting them to make broad tunnel frameworks that give asylum from hunters and natural limits.

The usefulness of the monster armadillo's hooks stretches out past tunnel uncovering to incorporate scavenging for underground food sources. Utilizing its sharp feeling of smell, the goliath armadillo finds bugs, hatchlings, and tubers underneath the dirt, utilizing its hooks to dig and uncover these secret luxuries. This specific transformation features the significance of paws in tending to the extraordinary difficulties of life in the prairies, where admittance to underground assets turns into a critical determinant of endurance.

Venturing into the freezing scenes of the Cold and subarctic districts, the polar bear (Ursus maritimus) arises as a famous monster of the mauled domain. Adjusted to an existence of ice and ocean, the polar bear's strong appendages and sharp paws are pivotal for exploring its cold climate and getting prey. While not as long as the paws of their earthy colored bear family members, the hooks of polar bears are bold and appropriate for grasping onto the elusive surfaces of ice floes.

The usefulness of polar bear hooks is generally obvious during their quest for seals, their essential prey. Polar bears utilize their sharp paws to make openings in the ice, calmly trusting that seals will surface for air. At the point when a seal shows up, the bear sends its paws to get a strong grasp and take the prey onto the ice. The paws likewise assume a part in climbing, supporting polar bears in scaling steep and frosty surfaces looking for prey or to get to reasonable resting spots. The flexibility of polar bear paws to the difficulties of their cold natural surroundings highlights the nuanced connection among structure and capability in the development of these designs.

In the distant rainforests of Southeast Asia, the sun bear (Helarctos malayanus) arises as a mauled monster with a novel arrangement of variations. Sun bears, the littlest among bear species, have sharp, non-retractable hooks that are appropriate for climbing trees and removing bugs from bark.

The usefulness of sun bear hooks is intently attached to their arboreal way of life, permitting them to get to in any case out of reach food sources in the thick timberland shade.

The paws of sun bears likewise assume a part in building homes in trees for resting and dozing. The bears utilize their sharp paws to tear and control branches, meshing them into improvised stages high over the timberland floor. This conduct gives a solid vantage point as well as helps sun bears stay away from ground-based hunters. The flexibility of sun bear paws to both scavenging and arboreal exercises features the adaptability of these designs in tending to the diverse difficulties of life in the rainforest.

Changing to the dry scenes of North America, the desert-staying Gila beast (Heloderma suspectum) arises as a ripped at goliath among reptiles. Regardless of its somewhat little size, the Gila beast has heavy appendages and sharp hooks, which are transformations for digging and tunneling in desert soils. The usefulness of Gila beast hooks is critical for making underground asylums, giving insurance from outrageous temperatures and expected hunters.

Gila beasts are fundamentally lone and crepuscular, rising up out of their tunnels to search for food during the cooler hours of the day. The hooks assume a part in unearthing tunnels, permitting Gila beasts to look for shelter and ration energy during the brutal intensity of the desert. Moreover, the paws help in their searching ways of behaving, as Gila beasts use them to attack homes of bird eggs or to find little vertebrates. The versatile meaning of Gila beast hooks lies in their commitment to the reptile's endurance in dry conditions, where admittance to underground shelters is fundamental for staying away from temperature limits.

In the rambling savannas and fields of Africa, the African elephant (Loxodonta africana) stands apart as a pawed monster with a one of a kind arrangement of transformations. Notwithstanding their gigantic size and the shortfall of customary paws, elephants have adjusted structures known as toenails, which serve comparative capabilities regarding usefulness. The toenails of elephants are significant for digging, scrounging, and even guard.

The usefulness of elephant toenails becomes clear during exercises like searching for water in dry riverbeds. Elephants utilize their forelimbs and toenails to make openings in the ground, arriving at underground water sources during times of dry season. Similar toenails are likewise utilized for evacuating plants, taking bark from trees, and controlling items in their current circumstance. Notwithstanding their utilitarian capabilities, elephant toenails assume a part in the perplexing social ways of behaving of these creatures, adding to correspondence through ground vibrations and checking.

The transformative meaning of elephant toenails lies in their versatility to the environmental difficulties of the African savanna. As herbivores with complex social designs, elephants have developed a bunch of devices — yet changed from customary hooks — that permit them to flourish in their sweeping and dynamic natural surroundings.

The nuanced connection among elephants and their current circumstance highlights the assorted manners by which paws, in different structures, add to the endurance and progress of species across various taxa.

In the beach front waters of the Southern Side of the equator, the New Zealand ocean lion (Phocarctos hookeri) arises as a mauled goliath among marine vertebrates. Known for their dexterity in both water and ashore, New Zealand ocean lions have sharp hooks on their forelimbs, which help in their developments on rough coastlines. The usefulness of these paws becomes vital during exercises, for example, pulling out onto land, exploring rough territory, and laying out regions.

New Zealand ocean lions are known for their momentous capacity to move quickly ashore notwithstanding their huge size. The sharp paws, related to strong appendages, permit them to navigate rough surfaces with deftness, making them very much adjusted to the seaside conditions they possess. The hooks likewise assume a part in cooperations between people, adding to showcases of predominance and regional protection. The flexibility of New Zealand ocean lion hooks to both earthbound and marine conditions features the transformative adaptability of these designs in tending to the difficulties of dynamic beach front environments.

In the many-sided embroidery of the ripped at domain, these goliaths, crossing different living spaces and scientific classifications, feature the versatile meaning of paws with regards to their particular environmental specialties. Whether it's the wolverine's ability in digging through snow, the polar bear's capacity to explore frigid scenes, or the sun bear's dexterity in the rainforest overhang, every species has advanced extraordinary paw variations that add to their endurance and outcome in their particular surroundings.

Past their nearby usefulness, the paws of these monsters hold social and representative importance. In different societies, these animals are adored as images of solidarity, strength, and the unpredictable dance among hunter and prey. The structure and capability of their hooks resound with human minds, starting both interest and, now and again, dread. The investigation of these tore monsters gives significant bits of knowledge into the complicated connections among organic entities and their surroundings, underscoring the nuanced manners by which development shapes the variety of life on The planet.

2.1: Apex Predators with Formidable Claws

Dominant hunters, possessing the apex of their particular pecking orders, frequently employ considerable paws as key instruments for endurance, predation, and biological strength. These animals, through the complicated dance of advancement, have created particular paws that add to their ruthless ability, empowering them to explore their surroundings, catch prey, and lay out strength inside their environments.

From the famous felids to the strong flying predators, the different cluster of dominant hunters grandstands the transformative creativity of hooks as multifunctional variations.

In the thick wildernesses of South America, the puma (Panthera onca) arises as a preeminent cat hunter, prestigious for its secrecy, strength, and well honed paws. Panthers are furnished with vigorous appendages and retractable paws, taking into account exact and quiet developments through their forested environments. The usefulness of puma paws is generally obvious during hunting undertakings, where these dominant hunters use a mix of secrecy and snare strategies.

The retractable idea of puma paws is a particular element among huge felines, offering a few benefits during the chase. Retractable hooks stay sheathed when not being used, saving their sharpness and limiting erosion with the ground. While following prey, panthers subtly approach their objective with unsheathed hooks, prepared to execute a quick and strong strike. The versatility of puma paws to various territories, from thick timberlands to open meadows, highlights their developmental importance in the complex scenes they occupy.

Puma paws likewise assume a vital part in the catch and dispatch of prey. During the last snapshots of an effective chase, pumas utilize their strong forelimbs and sharp hooks to convey an exact chomp to the skull or neck of their prey, guaranteeing a quick and productive kill. The usefulness of panther paws stretches out past predation to incorporate moving, as these huge felines are known to scale trees to get away from floods, stay away from hunters, or reserve prey in a protected area.

In the far reaching fields and savannas of Africa, the African lion (Panthera leo) remains as a notable dominant hunter with imposing hooks that supplement its social and agreeable hunting methodologies. Lions have sharp, retractable paws on their strong appendages, which they convey during different periods of the hunting system. The usefulness of lion hooks is fundamental to the outcome of gathering chases, an exceptional part of their social design.

During the following period of a chase, lions utilize their unsheathed paws to hold the ground quietly, limiting commotion and forestalling discovery by prey. The retractable idea of their paws permits lions to keep up with sharpness for the crucial point in time when the chase comes full circle in a run and last jump. The flexibility of lion paws to various kinds of territory, from open fields to thick vegetation, adds to the adaptability of these dominant hunters in assorted environments.

The cooperative idea of lion chases depends on the synchronized endeavors of pride individuals, with every individual contributing their one of a kind abilities, including the utilization of paws. Whenever prey is caught, the strong hooks of lions assume a pivotal part in quelling and dispatching the objective. This helpful hunting methodology, worked with by considerable paws, highlights the versatility of dominant hunters to various natural difficulties and prey types.

Wandering into the boreal woodlands and tundra districts of North America, the dim wolf (Canis lupus) arises as a dominant hunter with a social construction that depends on helpful hunting and the specific utilization of hooks. Wolves, portrayed areas of strength for by elements, have sharp, non-retractable paws adjusted for both hunting and other fundamental exercises. The usefulness of wolf hooks is intently attached to their job in seeking after, catching, and consuming prey.

Wolves utilize their hooks for digging, a way of behaving that fills numerous needs. The development of caves for raising posterity, the removal of reserves for putting away food, and the making of concealing spots for harmed or weak pack individuals all depend on the usefulness of wolf paws. The versatility of these hooks to different substrates, including soil, snow, and vegetation, features their part in tending to the assorted natural difficulties experienced by wolves in their broad regions.

During chases, wolves utilize their paws in a joint effort with their strong jaws to cut down prey. The quest for ungulates, like elk or caribou, includes key collaboration, with individual wolves adding to the pursuit and takedown. The grasping activity of wolf hooks supports keeping up with equilibrium and control during rapid pursuits, taking into account exact moves and facilitated endeavors inside the pack. The transformative meaning of wolf paws lies in their commitment to the helpful procedures that have permitted these dominant hunters to flourish in a scope of environments.

Changing to the aeronautical domain, the brilliant falcon (Aquila chrysaetos) stands apart as a dominant hunter among flying predators, eminent for its strong claws and imposing paws. Brilliant hawks have sharp, bended claws on areas of strength for them, adjusted for catching and stifling various prey, including little well evolved creatures and birds. The usefulness of these claws is basic to the hunting methodologies utilized by brilliant falcons in their extensive domains.

Brilliant hawks utilize a mix of sharp bills and strong claws during hunting campaigns. Their sharp vision permits them to recognize possible prey from huge spans, and when an objective is distinguished, the falcons utilize their imposing paws to execute quick and exact strikes. The grasping activity of brilliant falcon claws is worked with by sharp claw tips areas of strength for and muscles, guaranteeing a safe hang on prey during flight and forestalling escape.

The usefulness of brilliant falcon claws stretches out to their part in regional protection and connection with different hawks. During conflicts or shows of predominance, hawks might utilize their claws to wrestle with rivals, displaying the significance of these designs in both predation and interspecific rivalry. The versatility of brilliant bird claws to different environmental jobs supports their status as dominant hunters equipped for flourishing in various living spaces.

Directing our concentration toward the marine climate, the executioner whale (Orcinus orca) arises as a dominant hunter with a mix of knowledge, social construction, and strong forelimbs embellished with imposing paws. Executioner whales, otherwise called orcas, have a place with the dolphin family and are portrayed by their unmistakable highly contrasting tinge. Their hooks, however not apparent remotely like those of earthbound hunters, are available as minimal designs known as phalanges inside their flippers.

The usefulness of executioner whale paws, or phalanges, lies in their commitment to the complicated social ways of behaving and hunting systems of these dominant hunters. Executioner whales are known for their agreeable hunting methods, where people cooperate to target and curb prey, like seals, ocean lions, and, surprisingly, enormous whales. The flippers, lodging these minimal hooks, assume an essential part in crowding, corralling, and some of the time shocking prey during composed chases.

The versatility of executioner whale phalanges to social associations stretches out past hunting to incorporate presentations of correspondence, order, and familial securities. These designs, however not generally so remotely apparent as the hooks of earthly hunters, feature the adaptability of transformations inside the marine domain. The developmental meaning of executioner whale phalanges lies in their commitment to the biological achievement and flexibility of these dominant hunters in different maritime conditions.

In the underground scenes of North America, the fossorial star-nosed mole (Condylura cristata) arises as a charming dominant hunter with specific forelimbs and remarkable paw transformations. These little well evolved creatures, with a particular star-molded limb on their noses, have strong forelimbs outfitted with sharp paws adjusted for tunneling and hunting. The usefulness of star-nosed mole hooks is fundamental to their endurance in underground conditions.

Star-nosed moles utilize their sharp paws to unearth tunnels, making complex passage frameworks underneath the dirt. The versatility of these hooks to various kinds of soil, including thick and compacted substrates, permits star-nosed moles to explore productively through their underground natural surroundings. The usefulness of their paws likewise reaches out to scrounging for little spineless creatures, their essential prey, as they utilize the hooks to dig, test, and control the dirt looking for food.

The star-formed limb on their noses, related to their sharp hooks, upgrades the material feelings of star-nosed moles. The paws help in the investigation of their environmental elements and the identification of prey through touch. This exceptional variation grandstands the nuanced manners by which hooks add to tangible capabilities notwithstanding their job in tunneling and predation. The developmental meaning of star-nosed mole hooks lies in their particular variations for flourishing in underground biological systems.

In the parched scenes of North America, the famous desert-abiding diamondback (Crotalus spp.) addresses a dominant hunter among reptiles, outfitted with particular toxin infusing teeth and imposing hooks. However not apparent remotely, the paws of diamondbacks are addressed by bended, empty teeth situated in their upper jaws. The usefulness of these teeth is fundamental to the predation and environmental jobs of diamondbacks in their living spaces.

Diamondbacks utilize their imposing teeth to infuse toxin into prey, immobilizing and stifling it before utilization. The variation of empty teeth takes into consideration the effective conveyance of toxin, a vital part of their savage methodology. The usefulness of diamondback teeth is intently attached to their job as trap hunters, ready to pounce for clueless prey to pass by prior to conveying a fast and exact strike.

The flexibility of diamondback teeth to different prey types, including little well evolved creatures and birds, grandstands the adaptability of these designs in tending to the dietary necessities of these dominant hunters. Moreover, poisonous snake teeth assume a part in safeguard against expected dangers. When compromised, diamondbacks might strike protectively, utilizing their teeth to discourage hunters or saw risks. The developmental meaning of poisonous snake teeth lies in their specialization for both predation and self-protection in the parched environments they possess.

In the mind boggling woven artwork of dominant hunters, from earthbound scenes to the sea profundities, the consistent idea is the transformative creativity of imposing hooks. Whether it's the secretive and exact strikes of enormous felines, the helpful hunting systems of wolves, the strong claws of falcons, or the venomous teeth of snakes, every transformation serves a particular natural job in the endurance and outcome of these dominant hunters. The flexibility of paws, whether retractable, non-retractable, or minimal, highlights the versatility of creatures to different conditions and natural specialties.

In addition, the developmental meaning of hooks reaches out past their nearby usefulness to incorporate social and emblematic aspects. Dominant hunters frequently hold a respected status in human societies, filling in as images of solidarity, dexterity, and the multifaceted equilibrium of nature. The symbolism of hooks, whether portrayed in craftsmanship, folklore, or imagery, resounds with the base impulses and interest implanted in the human mind.

As stewards of the planet, understanding the job of dominant hunters and their impressive paws is significant for preservation endeavors and environmental equilibrium. The mind boggling connections between dominant hunters and their surroundings highlight the interconnected trap of life, where every species, outfitted with its remarkable variations, adds to the intricacy and strength of environments. In a quickly impacting world, the review and enthusiasm for dominant hunters and their impressive paws offer important experiences into the fragile dance among hunters and prey, development and transformation, and the persevering through marvels of the regular world.

Proceeding with our investigation of dominant hunters with impressive paws, we dig into the maritime domain to experience the extraordinary white shark (Carcharodon carcharias). The extraordinary white shark, frequently viewed as the sea's dominant hunter, has a bunch of momentous transformations, including strong jaws and serrated teeth that capability as imposing paws in the oceanic climate.

The usefulness of the extraordinary white shark's teeth is key to its job as a dominant hunter in marine environments. These sharks have columns of huge, serrated teeth that are appropriate for holding and tearing prey. The flexibility of their teeth to different prey things, going from seals to fish, features the adaptability of their ruthless techniques. Dissimilar to earthbound hunters, the incredible white shark's teeth are not utilized for biting; all things considered, they effectively cause handicapping nibbles for prey, starting a ruthless succession known as the "chomp and spit" technique.

The chomp and spit system includes the shark taking a strong nibble to immobilize or debilitate its prey. After the underlying nibble, the incredible white shark frequently delivers its hold, permitting the prey to debilitate or drain out prior to getting back to consume it. This technique limits the gamble of injury to the shark during possibly hazardous experiences with huge and strong prey. The flexibility of the extraordinary white shark's dental design to this ruthless methodology highlights the transformative meaning of teeth as particular apparatuses for hunting in the oceanic domain.

Past predation, the usefulness of the incredible white shark's teeth reaches out to social collaborations and correspondence. In regional debates or during mating experiences, sharks might involve their teeth in showcases of predominance or hostility. The serrated idea of the teeth fills in as a visual and material hindrance, building up the social order among people.

Changing to the perfect inverse of the marine climate, the strong and mysterious dominant hunter known as the snow panther (Panthera uncia) meanders the rough hilly scenes of Focal and South Asia. Notwithstanding its tricky nature, the snow panther has considerable paws that add to its endurance in the cruel and unforgiving high-elevation conditions.

The usefulness of the snow panther's paws is intently attached to its transformations for crossing steep and rough territory. These huge felines have strong appendages and non-retractable paws that give footing on rough surfaces, empowering them to explore bluffs and abrupt slants with unmatched spryness. The flexibility of snow panther hooks to the difficulties of their living space exhibits the job of these designs in tending to the one of a kind biological specialties involved by dominant hunters.

Snow panthers utilize their paws for movement as well as for hunting in the difficult conditions they occupy.

Going after blue sheep, Himalayan tahr, and different ungulates adjusted to rocky territory, snow panthers convey their strong appendages and sharp hooks to snare and quell prey. The usefulness of their paws in grasping and getting prey is urgent for the outcome of these secretive trackers in their high-height territories.

The subtle idea of snow panthers, combined with their variations for endurance, adds a layer of secret and worship to their social and representative importance. In different societies, these large felines are related with legendary and otherworldly traits, typifying the versatility and flexibility expected to flourish in outrageous conditions.

Traveling to the savannas and fields of Australia, the dominant hunter known as the Tasmanian demon (Sarcophilus harrisii) arises as a marsupial carnivore with one of a kind transformations, including strong jaws major areas of strength for and outfitted with considerable hooks. Regardless of its generally little size, the Tasmanian fiend is an imposing hunter with a searching way of life, using its powerful appendages and sharp hooks for different natural jobs.

The usefulness of Tasmanian villain paws is obvious in their digging conduct, which fills different needs. Villains utilize their paws to exhume tunnels for cover and settling, exhibiting their flexibility to earthly conditions. Furthermore, their paws help in scrounging for food, as Tasmanian demons rummage on carcass, little well evolved creatures, and birds. The flexibility of their paws to both digging and scrounging highlights the adaptability of these dominant hunters in different environments.

The Tasmanian fiend's social ways of behaving and cooperations further feature the usefulness of hooks. During conflicts or benefiting from bodies, people might involve their hooks in showcases of strength or guard. The flexibility of Tasmanian villain paws to social collaborations supplements their single and once in a while forceful nature, adding to their endurance in the powerful environments they possess.

Moving our concentration to the Icy and subarctic locales, the dominant hunter known as the wolverine (gulo) wanders the immense and snow-covered scenes, equipped with strong appendages and sharp, non-retractable paws. Wolverines, notwithstanding their humble size contrasted with other dominant hunters, have a bunch of transformations that incorporates considerable hooks pivotal for endurance in brutal conditions.

The usefulness of wolverine paws is noticeably shown in their digging conduct. Wolverines are achieved diggers, utilizing their sharp hooks to unearth through thick snowpack looking for food, like remains or little warm blooded creatures. Their versatility to diving in snow highlights the significance of hooks in tending to the difficulties of subarctic scenes, where admittance to prey and rummaging potential open doors might be restricted.

Wolverines likewise utilize their hooks for checking regions, leaving unmistakable fragrance marks on trees and shakes. This conduct is important for their correspondence methodology, permitting people to lay out and protect their reaches in the immense and frequently scantily populated Cold regions. The versatility of wolverine hooks to both digging and correspondence grandstands the multifunctionality of these designs in tending to the natural requests of dominant hunters in outrageous conditions.

In the tremendous and complex biological systems of the Amazon rainforest, the jaguarundi (Panther yagouaroundi) arises as a less popular however similarly captivating dominant hunter. This little wild feline, known for its slim form and prolonged body, has retractable paws that assume a pivotal part in its arboreal way of life and hunting systems.

The usefulness of jaguarundi paws is intently attached to their capacity to climb trees with readiness. Not at all like other enormous felines that are fundamentally earthbound, jaguarundis are talented climbers, utilizing their retractable hooks to explore the thick shade of the rainforest. The flexibility of their hooks to climbing exhibits the adaptability of these little dominant hunters in getting to arboreal conditions and hunting prey in the treetops.

Jaguarundis utilize their hooks for both predation and correspondence. Chasing after prey, they convey their retractable hooks to hold branches and explore the complicated organization of trees. Furthermore, during social cooperations or conflicts, people might involve their hooks for the purpose of correspondence, accentuating their versatility to the intricacies of rainforest biological systems.

These assorted instances of dominant hunters with imposing hooks highlight the flexibility and adaptability of these designs across various environments and species. From the sea profundities to high-height mountains, and from the savannas to thick rainforests, dominant hunters have developed paws that are finely tuned to address the particular difficulties of their surroundings.

Past their nearby usefulness, the paws of dominant hunters hold social and representative importance. In different societies, these animals are loved as images of solidarity, flexibility, and the complex dance among hunter and prey. The symbolism of hooks, whether portrayed in workmanship, folklore, or imagery, resounds with the basic impulses and interest implanted in the human mind.

As we keep on investigating the marvels of dominant hunters and their imposing paws, it becomes apparent that these variations are apparatuses for endurance as well as essential parts of the perplexing snare of life. Understanding the job of dominant hunters in biological systems is essential for preservation endeavors and keeping up with natural equilibrium. The review and enthusiasm for these wonderful animals offer important experiences into the fragile connections that shape the variety and flexibility of life on The planet.

2.2: Hunting Techniques and Adaptations

Hunting strategies and transformations among different species in the set of all animals are entrancing articulations of developmental resourcefulness. These procedures have developed over centuries, molding the endurance and progress of assorted creatures. From the secretive moves of enormous felines to the helpful hunting strategies of social hunters, and from the flying ability of flying predators to the specific procedures of marine trackers, the range of hunting variations grandstands the variety of life on The planet.

In the rich rainforests of South America, the puma (Panthera onca) rules as a preeminent hunter, epitomizing the specialty of secrecy and accuracy in hunting. Panthers have fostered a scope of transformations that make them imposing hunters in the thick vegetation of their living spaces. One key variation is their particular spotted coat, which goes about as viable cover in the midst of the dappled daylight sifting through the backwoods shelter. This transformation permits panthers to mix consistently into their environmental elements, improving their capacity to move toward prey undetected.

Pumas are additionally proficient swimmers, and their hunting strategies frequently include amphibian pursuits. Streams and streams jumbling the rainforest furnish panthers with the chance to snare prey from the water's edge. Their strong jaws, intended for a strong nibble, empower them to get a handle on and immobilize an assortment of prey, including capybaras, caimans, and boa constrictors. The flexibility of panther hunting methods to both earthbound and oceanic conditions features their adaptability and capacity to take advantage of various natural specialties inside their living space.

In the African savannas, the African lion (Panthera leo) exhibits an alternate arrangement of hunting procedures formed by its social design. Lions are notable for their helpful hunting procedures, depending on facilitated endeavors inside a pride to cut down enormous prey. The versatility of lions to bunch hunting is intently attached to areas of strength for them securities and correspondence inside the pride.

The hunting system commonly starts with a planned way to deal with following prey. Lions use cover and landscape to get as close as conceivable to their expected objective without being identified. Once ready, they execute a synchronized charge, using their strong appendages and sharp paws for an eruption of speed. The co-operative idea of the assault is a demonstration of the flexibility of lions to social hunting procedures, guaranteeing a higher achievement rate while bringing down bigger prey.

The lion's strong jaws and retractable hooks assume essential parts during the last phases of a chase. Lions hold back nothing or gag of their prey, conveying a stifling chomp to cut it down rapidly.

The retractable idea of their paws limits commotion during the methodology, keeping a component of shock. The flexibility of lions to both performance and gathering hunting, contingent upon the size and sort of prey, features the adaptability of their hunting methods in powerful savanna environments.

In the Icy tundra, the dominant hunter known as the polar bear (Ursus maritimus) exhibits hunting variations custom-made to its frosty natural surroundings. Polar bears are essentially savage, with seals being their fundamental prey. One of the striking variations of polar bears is their capacity to cover tremendous distances on ocean ice, utilizing their sharp feeling of smell to identify seals' breathing openings.

The polar bear's hunting procedure frequently includes tolerance and covertness. Utilizing their strong appendages and paws, they stand by without complaining close to seal breathing openings, here and there staying unmoving for broadened periods. At the point when a seal surfaces to inhale, the bear utilizes its sharp paws to make an opening in the ice and quickly maneuvers the seal onto the surface. This hunting methodology depends on the polar bear's versatility to the occasional vacillations of Icy ocean ice.

The particular variation of polar bear hooks, heavy and appropriate for grasping onto elusive surfaces, supplements their hunting method on ice. The paws, alongside strong appendages, empower polar bears to explore the difficult Cold climate and secure their essential food source. The versatility of polar bear hunting strategies to the powerful states of ocean ice highlights the transformative ability of these dominant hunters.

Changing to the ethereal domain, flying predators, like the peregrine hawk (Falco peregrinus), utilize hunting methods that feature their authority of the skies. Peregrine birds of prey are famous for their extraordinary speed and ethereal aerobatic exhibition, attributes that are essential to their hunting methodologies. Their flexibility to different conditions, from metropolitan regions to bumpy districts, is a demonstration of their flexible hunting methods.

One of the remarkable hunting variations of peregrine hawks is their high velocity stoop, a quick, vertical jump executed during the quest for prey. The bird of prey takes off to extraordinary elevations, then, at that point, tucks its wings and plunges toward its objective, arriving at speeds that can surpass 240 miles each hour. The stoop empowers the peregrine hawk to surround prey with mind boggling speed, involving its sharp claws and bended nose for an exact and deadly strike.

The flexibility of peregrine hawk hunting methods stretches out to metropolitan conditions, where they have been noticed hunting pigeons and different birds in thickly populated regions. In these settings, peregrine birds of prey use structures and designs as vantage focuses, displaying their capacity to adjust their hunting strategies to different scenes.

Their sharp vision and nimble ethereal moves, joined with impressive claws, make them considerable trackers fit for flourishing in different conditions.

Wandering into the marine domain, the executioner whale (Orcinus orca) addresses an exceptionally clever and socially complex dominant hunter with particular hunting strategies. Executioner whales, regardless of their name, are really the biggest individuals from the dolphin family and are known for their agreeable hunting procedures, frequently including particular methods relying upon the sort of prey.

One amazing hunting variation of executioner whales is their utilization of facilitated waves to oust seals from ice floes. In this strategy, a gathering of executioner whales swims as one, making waves that wash over the ice and possibly thump seals into the water. When the seals are in the water, the executioner whales send their strong tails and sharp teeth to get a feast. The flexibility of executioner whales to utilize helpful hunting strategies exhibits the significance of social designs in their prosperity as dominant hunters.

Executioner whales additionally show momentous versatility in hunting various types of whales. Certain populaces of executioner whales have created particular strategies for hunting bigger whales, including dark whales and baleen whales. These hunting techniques include composed assaults, with executioner whales cooperating to take advantage of weaknesses in the bigger whale's protections. The flexibility of executioner whale hunting procedures to various prey types features their adaptability and knowledge as dominant hunters in the maritime domain.

In the mind boggling embroidered artwork of the set of all animals, various variations in hunting methods mirror the perplexing exchange among hunters and their surroundings. From the secretive moves of earthly hunters to the aeronautical ability of birds and the helpful procedures of marine trackers, every species has advanced hunting methods that line up with its environmental specialty. These transformations are fundamental for getting food, laying an out area, and guaranteeing the endurance of the two people and populaces.

Past the quick usefulness of hunting variations, they likewise add to the more extensive natural equilibrium. Hunters assume an essential part in controlling prey populaces, forestalling overgrazing, and molding the dissemination of species inside biological systems. Understanding the subtleties of hunting procedures and variations gives significant bits of knowledge into the interconnected trap of life and the sensitive equilibrium that supports biodiversity.

As stewards of the planet, perceiving the significance of these variations is pivotal for preservation endeavors. Human exercises, for example, living space obliteration and environmental change, can affect the fragile harmony among hunters and prey. Protection drives that consider the environmental jobs of hunters and their hunting transformations add to the conservation of biodiversity and the strength of normal biological systems.

The huge range of hunting strategies and variations saw in the animals of the world collectively is a demonstration of the unimaginable variety of life on The planet. From the rainforests to the Icy tundra, and from the skies to the sea profundities, every species has advanced novel systems for obtaining food and guaranteeing its endurance. As we proceed to investigate and comprehend these transformations, we gain further experiences into the complexities of the normal world and our common obligation to shield its extravagance for people in the future.

2.3: Territorial Defense and Mating Displays

Regional protection and mating shows are entrancing ways of behaving displayed by a bunch of animal categories across the animals of the world collectively. These ways of behaving, formed by developmental tensions, assume critical parts in getting assets, laying out conceptive achievement, and guaranteeing the endurance of people and their posterity. From the mind boggling moves of birds of heaven to the strong thunders of enormous felines, and from the energetic presentations of fish in coral reefs to the regional markings of well evolved creatures, regional protection and mating shows exhibit the assorted manners by which organic entities explore their social and environmental scenes.

In the lavish rainforests of New Guinea, the extreme mating presentations of birds of heaven (Paradisaeidae) enrapture onlookers with their hypnotizing magnificence and intricacy. These avian miracles have advanced elaborate plumage, dynamic tones, and complicated dance schedules to draw in mates and lay out regenerative achievement. Mating shows among birds of heaven are not just stylish; they are finely tuned articulations of developmental variations.

One notable model is the brilliant bird of heaven (Lophorina superba), where guys take part in complicated romance moves to charm females. The male changes its appearance by spreading its ebony plumes into a cape, making an optical deception of a three-layered shape. This presentation, joined with synchronized developments and calls, fills in as a visual and hear-able display to draw in females. The versatility of these mating showcases to the rainforest climate mirrors the serious rivalry for mates and the need to hang out in an outwardly complicated scene.

Regional safeguard is one more pivotal part of avian way of behaving, and it is frequently interwoven with mating shows. Birds lay out and protect regions to get assets, including food, settling locales, and admittance to expected mates. The dynamic plumage and complicated shows displayed during regional safeguard fill double needs: drawing in likely mates and dissuading rival guys. This flexibility of conduct grandstands the essential harmony between drawing in mates and keeping an upper hand in the mind boggling elements of avian social orders.

Changing to the savannas of Africa, the lion (Panthera leo) stands apart as a famous illustration of regional protection and elaborate mating shows. Lions live in gatherings known as prides, where numerous females and their posterity exist together with an alliance of guys. The guys, known as alliance accomplices, cooperate to safeguard the pride's domain from rival guys.

Regional protection among lions includes vocalizations, aroma stamping, and incidental actual showdowns. Thundering is a conspicuous component of lion regional way of behaving, filling in as both a statement of presence and an admonition to likely gatecrashers. Lions use fragrance stamping, for example, pee showering and scratching on trees, to lay out and keep up with their regional limits. These ways of behaving are adaptably utilized to pass on data about the pride's size, strength, and conceptive status.

Mating shows among lions are frequently interwoven with regional elements. Male lions, after assuming control over a pride, may take part in presentations of predominance and insurance to protect mating potential open doors with the occupant females. The flexibility of these presentations mirrors the multifaceted exchange between regional safeguard, social construction, and regenerative outcome in lion prides.

Submerged domains, like coral reefs, have a variety of captivating regional safeguard and mating shows among marine organic entities. The energetic and various environment of coral reefs gives a phase to perplexing ways of behaving pointed toward getting mates and assets. One remarkable model is the romance and mating customs of reef fish, where versatility is critical to exploring the unique submerged climate.

The clownfish (Amphiprioninae), including the notable anemonefish, participate in intricate mating presentations and regional protection inside their ocean anemone homes. Male clownfish lay out regions inside the anemone and perform romance presentations to draw in females. The flexibility of their way of behaving incorporates enthusiastic swimming, balance shows, and complex body developments. When a couple frames, the female turns into the prevailing part, and the male adjusts to his job as a defensive mate and gatekeeper of their home.

Regional safeguard among reef fish includes ways of behaving, for example, pursuing interlopers, erupting blades, and vocalizations. The flexibility of these showcases is urgent for keeping up with the limits of a region inside the swarmed and serious climate of a coral reef. The multifaceted elements of mating showcases and regional guard among reef fish add to the strength and biodiversity of coral reef environments.

In the immense and different scenes of the Icy tundra, the caribou (Rangifer tarandus) represents regional protection and mating shows among well evolved creatures. Caribou, otherwise called reindeer in specific locales, structure enormous crowds that move across the tundra looking for food and appropriate calving grounds.

Regional protection in caribou is especially articulated during the rutting season, where guys take part in intricate presentations to vie for mates.

The flexibility of caribou mating shows includes vocalizations, tusk shows, and actual showdowns between rival guys. Male caribou develop tusks, which are shed and regrown every year, and use them as weapons during rivalries for predominance and admittance to females. The sound of prongs conflicting and the visual exhibition of guys locking horns are basic parts of caribou mating shows, displaying their flexibility to the difficult Cold climate.

Regional safeguard in caribou is frequently connected with the foundation and assurance of calving grounds. Guys effectively safeguard domains that give ideal circumstances to females to conceive an offspring and back their posterity. The versatility of these regional ways of behaving adds to the endurance and regenerative outcome of caribou groups in the unforgiving and eccentric Cold scenes.

In the broad meadows of North America, the buffalo (buffalo) shows regional ways of behaving that are profoundly imbued in their social construction and mating elements. Buffalo structure progressive social designs inside crowds, with prevailing guys getting mating open doors through showcases of solidarity and hostility.

Regional safeguard in buffalo includes actual showdowns, vocalizations, and presentations of predominance. Predominant guys, known as bulls, take part in forceful ways of behaving to lay out and keep up with their status inside the crowd. The versatility of these regional showcases incorporates pawing the ground, floundering in dust, and charging at rivals. These ways of behaving act as visual and olfactory signs of the bull's strength and regenerative wellness.

Mating shows among buffalo likewise include versatility as romance ways of behaving. Females, known as cows, may participate in specific mating inclinations in light of the presentations of predominance and strength showed by expected mates. The multifaceted dance between regional protection and mating shows in buffalo crowds mirrors the perplexing social elements that add to the conceptive achievement and endurance of the species.

In the perplexing embroidery of regional protection and mating shows, marine vertebrates offer enrapturing models in their maritime environments. Among cetaceans, the humpback whale (Megaptera novaeangliae) stands apart for its aerobatic presentations and complex melodies. These ways of behaving are striking instances of mating shows as well as act as key parts of social collaborations and correspondence inside humpback whale populaces.

Male humpback whales take part in intricate singing presentations during the mating season, delivering complicated and advancing examples of sounds. The versatility of these tunes includes individual variety and social transmission inside populaces.

The reason for humpback whale melodies is accepted to be connected to mate fascination and mate decision, with guys utilizing their vocalizations to impart their presence and wellness to females.

Regional protection among humpback whales is less articulated, as rivalry for mates ordinarily includes direct actual cooperations as opposed to laid out domains. Nonetheless, male humpback whales might participate in forceful ways of behaving, for example, tail slapping and penetrating, as a feature of their regenerative presentations. The versatility of these ways of behaving adds to the complicated social construction and reproducing elements of humpback whale populaces.

In the avian domain, the peacock (Pavo cristatus) is prestigious for its excessive plumage and complicated romance showcases. Local to South Asia, the peacock's energetic and radiant plumes assume a focal part in drawing in mates. The flexibility of peacock mating shows includes a mix of visual and hear-able components, making a tangible exhibition that is both staggering and powerful with regards to mate choice.

Male peafowls, known as peacocks, send their great tails in a fan-like showcase, uncovering a variety of lively quills with brilliant examples. The versatility of this show reaches out to going with vocalizations, including calls and shaking sounds created by the vibrations of their plume like quills. The synchronized blend of visual and hear-able prompts upgrades the general adequacy of peacock mating shows.

Regional safeguard among peafowls is less articulated contrasted with a few different animal categories, as their showcases are essentially centered around drawing in mates as opposed to hindering opponents. Notwithstanding, the versatility of peacock ways of behaving is clear in their capacity to lay out and protect regions where they take part in romance showcases. The mind boggling transaction between mating presentations and regional elements adds to the regenerative achievement and hereditary variety of peafowl populaces.

The versatility of regional protection and mating shows isn't restricted to earthbound conditions; it reaches out to the many-sided environments of coral reefs. Coral reef fish, for example, the clownfish referenced prior, take part in ways of behaving that are fundamental for getting mates and keeping up with regions inside the profoundly cutthroat reef climate. The versatility of these presentations is significant for exploring the difficulties of life on a coral reef.

An interesting model inside coral reef environments is the way of behaving of the mandarinfish (Synchiropus splendidus), known for its dynamic tones and mind boggling romance showcases. Mandarinfish are little, brilliantly shaded fish that occupy coral reefs in the Indo-Pacific district. During the mating season, male mandarinfish participate in intricate romance presentations to draw in females and lay out mating matches.

The flexibility of mandarinfish romance showcases includes synchronized swimming, unpredictable developments, and the introduction of dorsal and butt-centric blades with energetic varieties. These presentations are outwardly striking as well as act as signs of regenerative wellness and similarity. The flexibility of mandarinfish ways of behaving in exploring the mind boggling reef climate adds to the progress of their mating systems and the manageability of their populaces.

In the avian realm, the savvy grouse (Centrocercus urophasianus) offers a captivating illustration of regional guard and elaborate mating shows in North America. Sage-grouse are ground-abiding birds known for their mutual mating grounds, called leks, where guys participate in serious presentations to draw in females. The versatility of sage-grouse mating shows is necessary to their regenerative outcome in the sagebrush environments they possess.

Male sage-grouse accumulate in leks, where they show a mix of visual and hearable ways of behaving to lay out strength and draw in mates. The versatility of these presentations incorporates swelling air sacs, fanning tail feathers, and producing unmistakable sounds. The synchronized idea of sage-grouse shows inside leks makes a dynamic and serious air, permitting females to choose mates in view of the flexibility and life exhibited by showing guys.

Regional safeguard among sage-grouse is intently attached to the foundation and support of leks. Male sage-grouse safeguard explicit regions inside lek locales, and the flexibility of their ways of behaving includes forceful collaborations with rival guys. These regional elements add to the general outcome of sage-grouse mating methodologies and assume an essential part in forming populace elements inside sagebrush environments.

In the rambling scenes of the African savannas, the impala (Aepyceros melampus) grandstands regional guard and mating shows as essential parts of its social construction. Impalas, medium-sized gazelles, structure blended sex crowds, and guys participate in cutthroat presentations to lay out strength and secure mating open doors during the rearing season.

Regional protection among male impalas includes the foundation of domains inside the crowd's home reach. The flexibility of impala regional ways of behaving incorporates stamping an area limits with fragrance organs, taking part in vocalizations, and participating in actual presentations of strength. The versatility of these ways of behaving is pivotal for exploring the complicated elements of impala groups and accessing open females.

Mating shows among male impalas are portrayed by noteworthy a wide margin known as "pronking" or "stotting." The versatility of pronking includes a mix of high leaps and solid legged running, making an outwardly striking presentation of deftness and strength. Guys participate in pronking to draw in females, lay out predominance, and dissuade rival guys. The multifaceted exchange between regional protection and mating shows adds to the conceptive achievement and social elements of impala populaces in the savanna biological system.

The dim wolf (Canis lupus), a notable and exceptionally friendly carnivore, offers a convincing illustration of regional safeguard and helpful mating shows in North America, Eurasia, and portions of the Center East. Wolves live in family bunches called packs, where people take part in cooperative ways of behaving for hunting, an area protection, and raising posterity.

Regional safeguard among wolves includes vocalizations, fragrance stamping, and incidental actual showdowns with rival packs. Wolves utilize crying to impart over significant distances, supporting regional limits and planning pack developments. The flexibility of their vocalizations fills in as a critical part of pack elements, empowering productive correspondence in their sweeping domains.

Mating shows among wolves are described by romance ways of behaving and customs inside the pack. The alpha pair, frequently the rearing pair with laid out strength, may take part in holding ways of behaving, common prepping, and shared responsibilities regarding raising posterity. The versatility of helpful mating shows inside wolf packs adds to the solidness of social designs and the progress of their conceptive systems.

Regional protection and mating shows in the set of all animals are perplexing signs of transformative variations that guarantee the endurance and outcome of assorted species. Whether through energetic plumage, gymnastic romance ceremonies, or vocal showcases, creatures utilize a scope of systems to explore their social and environmental scenes. These ways of behaving are spellbinding to see as well as hold environmental importance, forming the elements of populaces and adding to the variety of life on The planet.

Past their nearby capabilities, regional safeguard and mating shows likewise offer important bits of knowledge into the complicated interaction between people, populaces, and environments. Understanding the flexibility of these ways of behaving gives a window into the sensitive equilibrium between rivalry and participation that oversees the regular world. As people proceed to study and value these captivating presentations, it turns out to be progressively clear that our stewardship of the planet includes perceiving and regarding the mind boggling dance of life unfurling in the bunch types of regional protection and mating shows across the animals of the world collectively.

2.4: The Ecological Impact of Clawed Giants

The natural effect of ripped at goliaths, incorporating a different scope of dominant hunters furnished with considerable paws, is a dynamic and vital part of biological systems all over the planet. These animals, frequently situated at the head of the pecking order, assume urgent parts in keeping up with environmental equilibrium, managing prey populaces, and forming the design of their particular natural surroundings.

From the profundities of the seas to the transcending pinnacles of mountains, and from the thick rainforests to the tremendous spans of meadows, mauled monsters use their transformations to leave a significant engraving on the perplexing trap of life.

In the marine domain, the orca, or executioner whale (Orcinus orca), stands apart as a tore goliath with massive environmental impact. Orcas are dominant hunters known for their knowledge, social intricacy, and imposing arrangement of teeth. Their natural effect reaches out past their immediate predation, shaping the way of behaving of prey species and impacting whole marine biological systems.

The versatility of orca hunting methods incorporates helpful methodologies utilized by unambiguous populaces to target huge prey, for example, baleen whales. Orcas have been noticed hunting in composed gatherings, with people showing specific jobs in disengaging, depleting, and eventually repressing their imposing prey. The versatility of their hunting methods grandstands the essential knowledge of orcas in exploring the difficulties of chasing after and catching enormous marine vertebrates.

The biological effect of orcas is further apparent in their capacity to direct prey populaces and keep up with environment balance. By going after seals, ocean lions, and certain whale species, orcas assist with controlling the wealth of these populaces, forestalling overgrazing of marine assets. This administrative job adds to the general wellbeing and strength of marine environments, underscoring the interconnectedness of hunter prey connections.

Conversely, the polar bear (Ursus maritimus), an earthbound hunter of the Cold, addresses a mauled monster with variations finely tuned to the difficulties of its frosty living space. The environmental effect of polar bears stretches out past their job as top hunters; they are essential to the elements of Cold food networks and the conservation of ocean ice biological systems.

Polar bears are particular trackers of seals, depending on ocean ice as a stage for hunting and getting to their essential prey. The flexibility of their hooks, appropriate for grasping onto dangerous surfaces, supplements their hunting procedure of delaying close to seal breathing openings and utilizing their strong appendages to maneuver seals onto the ice. The natural effect of polar bears on seal populaces adds to the guideline of marine biological systems, forestalling unrestrained development of seal populaces that could have flowing impacts on other Icy species.

The reliance of polar bears on ocean ice additionally features the biological effect of environmental change. The continuous decrease of Icy ocean ice because of an unnatural weather change represents a huge danger to polar bears, influencing their capacity to chase and access prey. The flexibility of polar bears to changing natural circumstances turns into a critical consider their environmental effect, as they explore the difficulties presented by a warming Cold.

In the huge fields of Africa, the African lion (Panthera leo) remains as a charming ripped at monster, forming the elements of savanna biological systems. Lions are social hunters that structure prides, comprising of numerous females and their posterity existing together with an alliance of guys. The natural effect of lions reaches out from their job as top hunters to their impact on herbivore conduct and vegetation structure.

Regional safeguard is a critical part of lion biology, and the flexibility of their ways of behaving incorporates vocalizations, fragrance checking, and periodic actual showdowns with rival prides. Lions lay out and safeguard domains, directing the overflow and conveyance of herbivores inside those areas. The flexibility of their regional elements adds to the steadiness of savanna biological systems, forestalling overgrazing and forming the sythesis of plant networks.

Mating shows among lions, entwined with regional elements, likewise assume a part in their biological effect. The versatility of their romance ways of behaving includes synchronized developments, vocalizations, and showcases of strength. Fruitful multiplication inside prides guarantees a nonstop presence of lions in the environment, adding to the guideline of herbivore populaces and keeping up with the sensitive harmony among hunters and prey.

The dark wolf (Canis lupus), a boundless hunter tracked down in different biological systems across North America, Eurasia, and portions of the Center East, addresses one more ripped at goliath with significant natural ramifications. Wolves are exceptionally friendly creatures that structure family bunches known as packs, and their natural effect reaches out from controlling prey populaces to impacting vegetation elements.

Regional guard among wolves includes vocalizations, fragrance stamping, and periodic actual showdowns with rival packs. The versatility of their regional ways of behaving adds to the foundation and upkeep of domains, controlling the overflow and conveyance of prey species inside those areas. The biological effect of wolves on prey populaces, for example, ungulates, forestalls overgrazing and shapes vegetation networks.

Helpful hunting systems, one more part of the biological effect of wolves, grand-stand the flexibility of their ways of behaving. Wolves chase in packs, utilizing composed strategies to target and stifle prey. This flexibility permits them to effectively bring down bigger prey species, adding to the guideline of herbivore populaces and impacting the design of environments.

In the Amazon rainforest, the puma (Panthera onca) arises as a strong ripped at goliath with a critical environmental effect. Panthers are lone hunters with a different eating routine that incorporates different earthbound and sea-going species. Their versatility to various territories inside the rainforest adds to their natural job as top hunters.

The flexibility of panther hunting methods incorporates following, ambushing, and protecting prey with strong jaws and sharp paws. Pumas are known to be capable swimmers, and their hunting strategies frequently include amphibian pursuits, for example, going after fish, caimans, and other sea-going species. The natural effect of panthers stretches out to managing populaces of herbivores and forestalling un-controlled development that could affect vegetation networks in the rainforest.

Panthers likewise assume an essential part in shaping the way of behaving of prey species. The simple presence of panthers in a space can impact the spatial and transient examples of herbivore action, known as the "scene of dread" impact. The flexibility of puma ways of behaving, including covert methodologies and trap strategies, adds to the complicated dance among hunters and prey, keeping an equilibrium in the mind boggling environments of the Amazon rainforest.

In the maritime domain, the extraordinary white shark (Carcharodon carcharias) features the biological effect of a considerable mauled goliath with transformations for hunting in marine conditions. Extraordinary white sharks are dominant hunters known for their strong jaws and serrated teeth, what capability as impressive paws in the amphibian domain. Their biological effect stretches out to directing marine populaces and affecting the way of behaving of prey species.

The flexibility of extraordinary white shark hunting procedures incorporates the "chomp and spit" methodology, where they convey strong nibbles to immobilize or weaken prey prior to getting back to consume it. This methodology limits the gamble of injury to the shark during experiences with huge and strong prey. The natural effect of extraordinary white sharks on marine environments includes keeping an equilibrium among marine animal categories and forestalling uncontrolled development of specific populaces.

The simple presence of extraordinary white sharks in marine conditions impacts the way of behaving of prey species, like seals and ocean lions. The flexibility of their ruthless systems adds to the "scene of dread" impact in the sea, molding the circulation and movement examples of marine well evolved creatures. The natural effect of extraordinary white sharks features their job as top hunters in keeping up with the wellbeing and flexibility of marine environments.

The Tasmanian fiend (Sarcophilus harrisii), a one of a kind marsupial meat eater tracked down in the timberlands and meadows of Tasmania, addresses a mauled goliath with a particular biological effect. The versatility of the Tasmanian demon to various territories highlights its job as a top hunter in the island's environments.

Tasmanian demons are known for their strong jaws and sharp teeth, adjusted for searching and hunting a different scope of prey.

The biological effect of Tasmanian villains stretches out to directing populaces of little warm blooded creatures, birds, and carcass. Their flexibility to various food sources permits them to assume a key part in keeping up with biological equilibrium inside Tasmania's different scenes.

One of the remarkable parts of the Tasmanian villain's environment is its rummaging conduct, consuming remains and adding to the disintegration of dead creatures. The flexibility of their taking care of propensities grandstands their environmental job as the two hunters and foragers, impacting supplement cycling and the general strength of biological systems.

In the avian domain, the shrew bird (Harpia harpyja) addresses a ripped at goliath with a huge natural effect in the neotropical rainforests of Focal and South America. Nag falcons are strong raptors known for their enormous size, solid claws, and imposing hunting abilities. Their environmental effect stretches out from managing populaces of arboreal warm blooded creatures to affecting the elements of rainforest biological systems.

The flexibility of shrew hawk hunting methods incorporates dexterous flight and exact claw strikes. Wench hawks are known for going after huge arboreal warm blooded animals, like monkeys and sloths, displaying their flexibility to hunting in the perplexing covering of rainforests. The biological effect of nag hawks includes controlling the populaces of these warm blooded creatures, forestalling overgrazing of vegetation and adding to the variety of rainforest environments.

Shrew falcons likewise assume a part in deeply shaping the way of behaving of prey species through their presence in the shade. The flexibility of their hunting ways of behaving impacts the dissemination and movement examples of arboreal well evolved creatures, making a "scene of dread" impact that adds to the equilibrium of hunter prey elements in the rainforest.

The environmental effect of pawed goliaths isn't restricted to coordinate predation; it additionally incorporates the more extensive impact these hunters have on the construction and working of biological systems. Dominant hunters, outfitted with impressive hooks or other specific variations, act as cornerstones in their particular living spaces. Their presence manages prey populaces, forestalls overgrazing, and adds to the general wellbeing and versatility of biological systems.

The flexibility of mauled monsters to different environments and biological specialties features their job as unique supporters of environment elements. From earthly hunters like lions and wolves to marine hunters like orcas and extraordinary white sharks, these pawed monsters are essential to the perplexing snare of life. As stewards of the planet, understanding and valuing the natural effect of these hunters is urgent for protection endeavors and the safeguarding of biodiversity.

The environmental effect of ripped at goliaths resounds across biological systems, molding the elements of hunter prey connections and affecting the design of natural surroundings. Whether in the profundities of the sea, the extensive savannas, or the thick rainforests, these dominant hunters add to the fragile equilibrium that supports life on The planet. As we dig further into the intricacies of natural communications, it turns out to be progressively clear that the flexibility of mauled monsters assumes an essential part in keeping up with the biodiversity and strength of our planet's different scenes.

Chapter 3

Claws as Tools for Survival

Hooks, advanced more than large number of years, stand as quintessential apparatuses for endurance across different species in the set of all animals. These versatile designs, made of keratin or chitin, serve different capabilities significant for getting food, safeguarding against hunters, laying out regions, and participating in complex social ways of behaving. From the imposing claws of raptors to the retractable hooks of enormous felines, and from the strong pliers of scavangers to the digging paws of tunneling warm blooded animals, the flexibility of hooks as devices for endurance highlights the momentous versatility of life on The planet.

In the avian domain, raptors embody the authority of paws as apparatuses for endurance. Flying predators, like birds, falcons, and hawks, employ sharp and strong claws intended for catching and getting prey. The versatility of raptor claws reaches out to their size, shape, and capability in light of the particular natural specialty of every species.

The essential capability of raptor claws is predation, and the flexibility of their design takes into consideration different hunting methods. Hawks, with huge and vigorous claws, are fit for seizing and diverting generally enormous prey, while birds of prey, with slim and sharp claws, depend on speed and accuracy to catch dexterous birds mid-flight.

The flexibility of these particular hunting devices guarantees the endurance and regenerative outcome of raptors inside their individual biological systems.

In the earthly domain, enormous felines, including lions, tigers, and cheetahs, exhibit the meaning of paws as apparatuses for endurance. These carnivores have retractable hooks, a developmental variation that upgrades their hunting ability. The versatility of retractable hooks permits huge felines to keep them sharp and safeguarded when not being used, lessening mileage and keeping up with their adequacy for hunting.

The essential capability of huge feline hooks is hunting and getting prey. The versatility of their hooks to various hunting methodologies is obvious in the following, jumping, and catching strategies utilized by these hunters. Lions, for instance, utilize their paws to wrestle with and stifle prey, while cheetahs depend on their hooks for footing during rapid pursuits. The versatility of enormous feline paws highlights their job in predation as well as in keeping away from pointless openness that could think twice about capacity to chase and make due.

Submerged, shellfish employ hooks with wonderful flexibility, filling in as multifunctional devices for endurance. Crabs, lobsters, and different shellfish utilize their paws for a scope of purposes, including catching prey, guarding against hunters, and laying out regions. The versatility of shellfish paws is exemplified by varieties in size, shape, and concentrated capabilities among various species.

Crab hooks, or chelae, fluctuate from species to species, reflecting variations to their particular surroundings and ways of behaving. Fiddler crabs, for example, show stamped sexual dimorphism in their hooks, with guys having one essentially bigger paw utilized in romance shows and flagging. The flexibility of these particular hooks upgrades the endurance chances of shellfish by giving instruments custom fitted to their environmental necessities, whether for taking care of, guard, or social communications.

In the domain of earthly warm blooded creatures, the aardvark (Orycteropus afer) grandstands the flexibility of hooks for endurance through digging. A nighttime, tunneling warm blooded creature local to Africa, the aardvark depends on its strong hooks to exhume tunnels for safe house and scrounging. The versatility of aardvark hooks to digging is fundamental for getting to subterranean insect and termite provinces, their essential food source.

The aardvark's hooks are hearty and appropriate for getting through hard soil and termite hills. The versatility of these digging instruments permits the aardvark to take advantage of a rich wellspring of sustenance while likewise giving security from hunters. The endurance outcome of the aardvark is intently attached to the versatility of its hooks, empowering it to flourish in various African territories.

In the oceanic domain, ocean otters (Enhydra lutris) exhibit the versatility of hooks as devices for endurance in a marine climate. Ocean otters have sharp and capable hooks on their forelimbs, which they use for preparing, controlling items, and getting prey. The flexibility of ocean otter paws is especially essential for their scavenging conduct, which includes catching and consuming different marine spineless creatures, including ocean imps, crabs, and shellfishes.

Ocean otters show noteworthy versatility in utilizing their hooks to open shells and concentrate meat from hard-to-arrive at fissure. The flexibility of their hooks as flexible devices permits ocean otters to take advantage of a different scope of prey species, adding to their endurance in the dynamic and testing marine environment. Also, the prepping conduct worked with by their hooks keeps up with their fur's protecting properties, fundamental for remaining light and warm in chilly sea waters.

In the extensive meadows of North America, the pronghorn (Antilocapra Yankee folklore) features the versatility of hooks for endurance through particular foot structures. While false hooks, the pronghorn's hooves are adjusted to serve explicit capabilities connected with their remarkable environmental specialty. The flexibility of pronghorn hooves adds to their uncommon speed and deftness, making them the quickest land well evolved creatures in North America.

Pronghorn hooves have a curved shape with a sharp external edge, giving foothold and grasp on different landscapes. The flexibility of their foot structure permits pronghorns to explore through different scenes, from open fields to rough lower regions. The method for surviving of pronghorns includes quick and dexterous development, and the flexibility of their hooves assumes a urgent part in dodging hunters and getting to assets.

In the bone-dry locales of Australia, the prickly villain (Moloch horridus) remains as a one of a kind reptilian illustration of hooks adjusted for endurance. Notwithstanding its name, the prickly villain is an innocuous reptile that depends on its particular hooks for effective development and endurance in brutal desert conditions. The versatility of prickly villain paws is clear in their job as effective apparatuses for tunneling, which assists the reptile with staying away from outrageous temperatures and hunters.

The prickly fallen angel's hooks are thin and adjusted to diving in sandy soils. The flexibility of these hooks permits the reptile to make tunnels that act as both sanctuary and security from temperature limits. Furthermore, the prickly demon's paws add to its scrounging methodology, as the reptile consumes subterranean insects by utilizing its particular tongue to catch them. The flexibility of prickly demon hooks mirrors the reptile's capacity to flourish in dry scenes by using tunneling as a method for surviving.

Paws as instruments for endurance address a remarkable illustration of transformative variation across a different exhibit of animal types.

From the skies to the profundities of the seas, and from earthbound scenes to dry deserts, the flexibility of paws highlights their fundamental job in getting food, safeguarding against hunters, and exploring complex environments. Whether utilized for predation, digging, climbing, or other particular capabilities, hooks add to the versatility and endurance of species in their separate territories. As we investigate and value the horde manners by which hooks have advanced, it becomes apparent that these amazing apparatuses are useful limbs as well as complicated arrangements created essentially to address the extraordinary difficulties of endurance in nature.

3.1: Prey Capture and Feeding Strategies

Prey catch and taking care of methodologies address a captivating and various part of the set of all animals, exhibiting the brilliant manners by which various species have developed to get food in their separate surroundings. From the covert methodologies of hunters to the channel taking care of procedures of amphibian creatures, and from the agreeable hunting systems of social hunters to the specific transformations for rummaging, the techniques utilized for catching and consuming prey mirror the extraordinary flexibility and genius of life on The planet.

In the tremendous and dynamic seas, marine hunters utilize different prey catch and taking care of systems adjusted to the difficulties of the submerged climate. The dominant hunter of the seas, the incredible white shark (Carcharodon carcharias), uses a mix of secrecy, speed, and strong jaws to catch prey. The incredible white shark utilizes a snare technique, frequently moving toward its prey from underneath and sending off a quick, strong assault to convey a lethal chomp.

The taking care of system of the incredible white shark includes holding onto prey with its serrated teeth, causing serious wounds that debilitate or kill the prey. The flexibility of its jaw structure permits the shark to make huge, strong chomps and consume various marine creatures, including seals, ocean lions, and fish. This taking care of procedure, set apart by exact and strong nibbles, is urgent for the extraordinary white shark's endurance as a top hunter in marine environments.

Conversely, channel taking care of living beings, for example, baleen whales, have advanced specific techniques to catch and consume immense measures of little creatures, essentially microscopic fish and little fish. Baleen whales, including species like the blue whale (Balaenoptera musculus), use brush like designs made of keratin, known as baleen plates, to channel food from the water.

The taking care of technique of baleen whales includes taking in huge pieces of water and afterward utilizing their tongue to push the water out through the baleen plates, catching little living beings simultaneously.

The flexibility of this channel taking care of method permits baleen whales to target thick fixes of prey, like krill, in an exceptionally productive way. The taking care of techniques of marine hunters and channel feeders represent the assorted manners by which organic entities have developed to take advantage of their seagoing conditions.

In earthbound conditions, enormous felines like lions (Panthera leo) feature a mix of secrecy, strength, and social collaboration in their prey catch and taking care of systems. Lions are social hunters that structure prides, comprising of numerous females and their posterity existing together with an alliance of guys. This social design upgrades their hunting achievement and considers agreeable techniques during prey catch.

The taking care of system of lions includes composed hunting endeavors, with people cooperating to seclude, tail, and at last repress prey. The flexibility of their social design permits lions to bring down bigger prey, like wildebeests and zebras, by overpowering them with composed assaults. The taking care of cycle inside the pride is various leveled, with prevailing people frequently having need admittance to the corpse.

One more noteworthy illustration of earthly prey catch and taking care of procedures is shown by the cheetah (Acinonyx jubatus), eminent for its extraordinary speed and deftness. The cheetah's taking care of system includes following and running to get prey, principally little to medium-sized ungulates. The flexibility of the cheetah's body structure, described by a lightweight form, specific respiratory and cardiovascular frameworks, and non-retractable paws, permits it to accomplish surprising velocities during short eruptions of running.

The cheetah's hunting technique frequently includes single pursuits, and when the prey is gotten, the cheetah utilizes its sharp hooks and strong jaws to cut it down. The taking care of cycle is quick, as different hunters or scroungers might represent a danger to the cheetah's kill. The flexibility of the cheetah's body and hunting techniques mirrors the transformative compromises vital for a profoundly specific and effective hunter.

In the far reaching meadows of North America, the pronghorn (Antilocapra History of the U.S) displays one of a kind variations for prey catch and taking care of. While not a hunter, the pronghorn is prestigious for its uncommon speed, making it the quickest land warm blooded creature in North America. The taking care of procedure of the pronghorn includes particular eating on various grasses, forbs, and bushes.

The flexibility of the pronghorn's taking care of system is set apart by its capacity to switch among perusing and brushing, contingent upon occasional food accessibility. The pronghorn's slim, forked horns are not utilized for catching prey but instead act as a protective transformation against hunters. The versatility of its taking care of ways of behaving permits the pronghorn to take advantage of assorted plant assets and explore the difficulties of its prairie territory.

In the complex environments of tropical rainforests, where thick vegetation can present difficulties for hunters, a few animal categories have developed extraordinary prey catch and taking care of methodologies. The nag bird (Harpia harpyja), a dominant hunter in neotropical rainforests, utilizes a mix of covertness, strong claws, serious areas of strength for and for prey catch. The wench bird's, major areas of strength for huge are adjusted for getting a handle on and conveying prey, frequently comprising of enormous arboreal vertebrates like monkeys and sloths.

The taking care of technique of the wench hawk includes roosting in raised positions, examining the environmental factors, and sending off shock assaults on clueless prey. The flexibility of its hunting strategies permits the shrew hawk to explore the perplexing covering of rainforests and secure prey in testing conditions. The shrew bird's job as a top hunter adds to the guideline of arboreal warm blooded creature populaces in rainforest biological systems.

In the domain of bugs, the supplicating mantis (Mantodea) represents an exceptional and particular way to deal with prey catch. The imploring mantis is a trap hunter with changed forelimbs adjusted for getting a handle on and holding prey. The taking care of procedure of the imploring mantis includes quietly holding up in a disguised situation until a clueless bug draws near striking reach.

The versatility of the supplicating mantis' forelimbs considers quick and exact developments to catch prey. When prey is reachable, the mantis utilizes its sharp spines to immobilize and consume it. The taking care of interaction might include the mantis consuming the prey while it is as yet alive. The flexibility of the imploring mantis' savage conduct grandstands the different techniques utilized by bugs for prey catch.

In the sea-going domain, cephalopods, including octopuses and squids, feature momentous variations for prey catch and taking care of. These exceptionally shrewd and lithe marine living beings have appendages furnished with suckers or particular arms with suckers, which they use to catch and control prey. The taking care of system of cephalopods includes dynamic hunting and, now and again, complex disguise procedures.

The versatility of cephalopod taking care of systems is obvious in their capacity to utilize various strategies for various prey. For instance, a few animal groups utilize their limbs to seize and immobilize prey, while others, similar to the copy octopus, utilize complicated mimicry to emulate the appearance and conduct of harmful creatures to stop hunters and catch prey. The flexibility of cephalopod taking care of ways of behaving features their mind boggling and adaptable way to deal with endurance in assorted marine conditions.

Rummaging, the demonstration of consuming flesh or disposed of remains, is one more predominant taking care of technique utilized by different species. Scroungers assume a vital part in biological systems by reusing supplements and limiting the development of bodies.

The versatility of scroungers to take advantage of accessible food assets adds to their outcome in assorted conditions.

The vulture, especially the griffon vulture (Cheats fulvus), is a striking scrounger with particular transformations for benefiting from remains. The taking care of methodology of vultures includes taking off high overhead, utilizing sharp visual perception to detect corpses. The versatility of their solid mouths and necks permits them to tear through intense stows away and access supplement rich tissues. Vultures assume an imperative environmental part by productively tidying up creature remains and forestalling the spread of infections.

In the cold and subarctic locales, the Icy fox (Vulpes lagopus) displays a rummaging procedure, depending on flesh and food stores left by different hunters. The versatility of the Cold fox to brutal and variable circumstances incorporates its capacity to effectively find and use food assets. Throughout the colder time of year, when prey accessibility is restricted, the Icy fox might search the remaining parts of bigger hunters' kills or feed on put away food.

The versatility of searching ways of behaving is likewise seen in the hyena, especially the spotted hyena (crocuta), which is known for its artful taking care of propensities. The taking care of procedure of hyenas includes a mix of hunting and rummaging, and they are known to consume an extensive variety of prey, including flesh, little vertebrates, and even plant material. The flexibility of their jaws and teeth permits hyenas to consume bones, giving them fundamental supplements not found in muscle tissues.

The different taking care of techniques utilized by hunters, herbivores, and scroungers mirror the perplexing trap of communications inside biological systems. The flexibility of these systems is many times formed by the environmental specialties in which species advance, affecting their life systems, ways of behaving, and social designs. As life forms explore the difficulties of securing and handling food, the variety of prey catch and taking care of methodologies turns into a demonstration of the noteworthy creativity of nature in maintaining life on earth.

3.2: Climbing and Navigational Abilities

Getting over and navigational capacities address fundamental transformations that empower different species to cross assorted scenes, from transcending trees to rough uneven territories. These capacities, sharpened through advancement, permit organic entities to get to assets, stay away from hunters, track down mates, and lay out domains. The flexibility of climbing and navigational methodologies is clear across the animals of the world collectively, exhibiting the surprising manners by which various species have advanced to address the difficulties of their surroundings.

In the lavish shelters of tropical rainforests, arboreal creatures display great climbing and navigational capacities, exhibiting transformations that empower them to flourish in the complex and in an upward direction arranged climate.

One noteworthy model is the bug monkey (Ateles spp.), known for its exceptional nimbleness in exploring the treetops. The prehensile tail of arachnid monkeys is a critical variation, giving them excellent equilibrium and control as they swing from one branch to another.

The versatility of arachnid monkey tails stretches out to their capacity to get a handle on and control objects, permitting them to explore the many-sided overhang proficiently. These monkeys show a skilled comprehension of their three-layered climate, using a blend of appendages and tail to drive themselves through the trees. Their climbing and navigational capacities are fundamental for getting to organic products, leaves, and different assets disseminated across the shade.

One more arboreal animal groups with wonderful climbing and navigational capacities is the gecko, known for its cement toe cushions that empower it to stick to vertical surfaces and even drop topsy turvy. The flexibility of gecko toe cushions is credited to infinitesimal designs called setae, which make glue powers through van der Waals connections. This momentous variation permits geckos to climb different surfaces, from smooth glass to unpleasant tree rind.

The climbing and navigational capacities of geckos stretch out past their glue toe cushions to incorporate specific ways of behaving like tail usage for balance and controlled drops. The flexibility of these climbing procedures is significant for geckos to get to raised areas, avoid hunters, and find prey. The capacity to explore assorted surfaces grandstands the flexibility of climbing transformations in arboreal conditions.

In the avian domain, a few animal varieties have developed uncommon climbing and navigational capacities to get to raised settling locales, dodge hunters, and find food sources. The woodpecker (Picidae family) is an eminent model, displaying a set-up of transformations for climbing and rummaging on trees. The versatility of the woodpecker's solid and etch formed bill permits it to exhume holes in tree trunks to get to bugs and hatchlings.

Woodpeckers additionally have specific feet with zygodactyl plan, including two toes pointing forward and two in reverse. This variation upgrades their abilities to climb by giving a protected grasp on vertical surfaces. The flexibility of woodpeckers to explore tree trunks and branches is supplemented by areas of strength for them feathers, which go about as a prop for dependability during climbing and examining for prey.

Getting over and navigational capacities are likewise significant for the endurance of species in uneven territories, where steep slants and tough scenes present remarkable difficulties. The ibex, a gathering of wild goats in uneven districts, represents flexibility to such conditions. The Elevated ibex (Capra ibex), for example, exhibits exceptional climbing skills that permit it to explore steep precipices and rough surfaces effortlessly.

The versatility of ibex climbing techniques incorporates particular hooves with curved undersides that give footing on rough territory. These hooves can be utilized like pull cups to stick to vertical surfaces, permitting the ibex to get to in any case blocked off regions looking for food and mates. The navigational capacities of ibexes in sloping scenes feature the flexibility of their physical elements to the difficulties presented by steep and rough conditions.

In the domain of reptiles, the chameleon is famous for its climbing and navigational capacities, especially its prehensile tail and concentrated feet. The flexibility of the chameleon's prehensile tail permits it to handle and fold over branches, giving solidness during climbing. Furthermore, the chameleon's zygodactyl feet with combined toes empower a protected hold on slim branches and twigs.

Chameleons are arboreal reptiles known for their capacity to change tone for correspondence, thermoregulation, and cover. The flexibility of their climbing and navigational methodologies is intently attached to their arboreal way of life, empowering them to move proficiently through vegetation looking for prey and mates. The blend of a prehensile tail, specific feet, and flexible variety changing capacities mirrors the chameleon's momentous versatility to arboreal conditions.

In oceanic conditions, exploring through water presents one of a kind difficulties, and a few animal groups have developed particular transformations for swimming and submerged development. The penguin, especially the Sovereign penguin (Aptenodytes forsteri), features wonderful navigational capacities in the water. The versatility of penguins to the oceanic domain incorporates smoothed out bodies, flipper-like wings, and webbed feet, permitting them to explore through the water proficiently.

Sovereign penguins, specifically, are known for their significant distance submerged searching excursions. The versatility of their swimming methodologies includes strong and composed developments of their flippers and body, permitting them to explore through sea flows looking for prey, fundamentally fish and squid. The navigational capacities of penguins in the water feature the flexibility of their physical elements to a semi-oceanic way of life.

Rather than the smoothed out groups of penguins, ocean turtles exhibit novel transformations for swimming and route. The flexibility of ocean turtle appendages to paddle-like flippers empowers them to explore through seas over huge distances. Ocean turtles are known for their astounding navigational capacities, especially during long movements to settling locales.

The versatility of ocean turtles' navigational techniques includes their capacity to recognize Earth's attractive field and use it for direction. This exceptional transformation permits them to explore across seas and return to explicit settling destinations with accuracy. The navigational capacities of ocean turtles are significant for their endurance, adding to effective generation and keeping up with populaces across various marine territories.

In the unpredictable environments of coral reefs, various marine organic entities exhibit flexibility to explore through complex designs and find appropriate natural surroundings. The clownfish (Amphiprioninae), known for its relationship with ocean anemones, shows navigational capacities inside the coral reef climate. The flexibility of clownfish to explore through coral arrangements includes retaining explicit courses and milestones to move productively and find cover.

Clownfish, especially the notable species like the ocellaris clownfish, grandstand anemone-facilitating conduct. The versatility of their navigational capacities permits them to find and perceive explicit anemones inside the complicated coral reef climate. Navigational abilities are essential for clownfish endurance, assisting them with keeping away from hunters, find food sources, and lay out domains inside the complexities of coral reef biological systems.

In the far reaching scenes of deserts, where outrageous temperatures and tremendous open spaces present difficulties, a few animal varieties have developed remarkable transformations for route and endurance. The desert insect (Cataglyphis spp.) is a wonderful model, exhibiting flexibility to explore across featureless territories and find food sources. The flexibility of desert insect route includes the utilization of heavenly signals, energized light examples, and visual recollections.

Desert insects are known for their productive scrounging conduct, frequently covering extensive distances looking for food. The flexibility of their navigational systems incorporates the capacity to utilize the place of the sun and examples of energized light overhead for direction. Furthermore, desert subterranean insects make visual recollections of their environmental factors, permitting them to precisely explore back to the home. The navigational capacities of desert subterranean insects feature the flexibility of tangible systems to the difficulties of deserts.

In the domain of well evolved creatures, the dim wolf (Canis lupus) embodies flexibility in exploring assorted scenes, from thick backwoods to open fields. Wolves are social hunters that frequently travel in packs, exhibiting agreeable hunting and navigational ways of behaving. The versatility of wolf pack elements includes correspondence through vocalizations, fragrance checking, and facilitated developments during hunting and domain route.

Wolves have a sharp feeling of smell, permitting them to recognize and follow fragrances over significant distances. The flexibility of their navigational capacities incorporates the utilization of aroma trails to find prey, speak with pack individuals, and lay out domain limits. The social construction and navigational methodologies of wolf packs add to their prosperity as dominant hunters in various biological systems.

In the multifaceted biological systems of mangrove timberlands, where land and water meet, species, for example, the proboscis monkey (Nasalis larvatus) grandstand flexibility in climbing and exploring through the extraordinary scene.

The versatility of the proboscis monkey's abilities to climb includes its long and solid appendages, prehensile tail, and concentrated feet for grasping branches.

Proboscis monkeys frequently travel through mangrove trees looking for food and appropriate natural surroundings. The versatility of their navigational methodologies incorporates a comprehension of the perplexing mangrove environment, permitting them to find taking care of regions and stay away from hunters. The remarkable life systems and conduct of proboscis monkeys feature their versatility to the difficulties of living in the unique connection point among land and water.

In the unpredictable biological systems of coral reefs, different marine life forms exhibit versatility to explore through complex designs and find reasonable natural surroundings. The clownfish (Amphiprioninae), known for its relationship with ocean anemones, shows navigational capacities inside the coral reef climate. The flexibility of clownfish to explore through coral developments includes remembering explicit courses and milestones to move effectively and find cover.

Clownfish, especially the notable species like the ocellaris clownfish, grandstand anemone-facilitating conduct. The versatility of their navigational capacities permits them to find and perceive explicit anemones inside the complicated coral reef climate. Navigational abilities are essential for clownfish endurance, assisting them with staying away from hunters, find food sources, and lay out regions inside the complexities of coral reef environments.

3.3: Self-Defense Mechanisms

Self-preservation instruments address an entrancing exhibit of variations that living beings across the set of all animals have created to shield themselves from hunters, contenders, or ecological dangers. These systems, sharpened through great many long stretches of development, include a large number of techniques, from actual transformations to social strategies. The flexibility of self-protection systems mirrors the different difficulties that living beings face in their particular environments and the brilliant manners by which they have advanced to guarantee their endurance.

In the domain of actual variations for self-preservation, the porcupine fills in as a striking model, exhibiting an impressive cluster of spines or plumes. The versatility of porcupine plumes lies in their changed design, highlighting spikes that make extraction troublesome once implanted in the skin of a hunter or danger. Porcupines can effectively protect themselves by turning their plume covered backs toward expected assailants, deflecting hunters with the danger of excruciating wounds.

The flexibility of porcupine self-preservation systems reaches out past actual elements to incorporate social techniques.

When undermined, porcupines may likewise produce cautioning sounds, chat their teeth, or even charge at hunters, using a blend of physical and social variations to dissuade possible dangers. The versatility of porcupine safeguards exhibits the combination of both primary and conduct components for successful self-conservation.

In the avian domain, the sharp followed quick (Zoonavena sylvatica) shows a novel self-protection system including particular plumes on its wings. These quills have solid spikes with sharp places, and when the quick is undermined, it can stretch out its wings to make an obstruction of sharp focuses around its body. The versatility of this actual safeguard is obvious in the quick's capacity to utilize its wings both for flight and as a defensive safeguard against possible hunters.

The sharp followed quick's self-protection system fills in as a hindrance to would-be aggressors, making it trying for hunters to approach or endeavor to catch the quick. The versatility of involving wings as a cautious boundary grandstands the combination of physical highlights for both streamlined capability and self-security in light of dangers.

In the far reaching scenes of Africa, the African elephant (Loxodonta africana) epitomizes the flexibility of actual guards for self-protection. African elephants are furnished with considerable tusks, prolonged incisor teeth that serve different capabilities, including self-protection. The versatility of elephant tusks stretches out to different purposes, like searching for water, taking bark from trees, and, urgently, hindering expected dangers.

Elephants utilize their tusks as strong weapons against hunters or saw risks. The flexibility of this actual guard component is especially apparent during conflicts with hunters, where elephants might utilize their tusks to charge, punch, or strike, successfully fighting off dangers. The flexibility of elephant tusks features the reconciliation of guarded highlights into day to day exercises, displaying their multifunctional job in endurance.

In the marine domain, the flexibility of self-protection systems is exemplified by the cuttlefish (Sepiida request). Cuttlefish have modern cover capacities that serve both for of keeping away from hunters and as a strategy for ambushing prey. The versatility of cuttlefish cover includes the capacity to quickly change the variety, example, and surface of their skin to match their environmental factors.

Cuttlefish utilize particular cells called chromatophores to control shades in their skin, permitting them to mix consistently into their current circumstance. This versatility in cover fills in as a visual obstacle against hunters, making it trying for them to recognize the cuttlefish as it explores through complex marine living spaces. The flexibility of cuttlefish disguise mirrors their authority of self-preservation in the dynamic and outwardly complex submerged world.

In the bug world, the bombardier bug (Carabidae family) grandstands a novel and compound based self-preservation component. At the point when undermined, the bombardier creepy crawly discharges a hot, poisonous compound splash from specific stomach organs, making an explosion of harmful fumes and launching it toward the danger. The versatility of this substance protection is because of the exact blending of reactant synthetics inside the bug's body, bringing about an exothermic response that delivers the poisonous splash.

The versatility of the bombardier scarab's substance guard fills in as both an obstruction and a method for security against hunters. The hot and burning nature of the shower hinders likely dangers, and the accuracy of the discharge system forestalls damage to the actual scarab. This self-protection system features the versatility of compound components in discouraging hunters and guaranteeing the scarab's endurance.

In the reptilian domain, the horned reptile (Phrynosoma spp.) shows a charming self-protection component including mimicry and actual variations. At the point when compromised, the horned reptile can expand its body, causing itself to seem bigger and more trying for hunters to swallow. The flexibility of this expansion safeguard fills in as a visual obstacle, discouraging hunters from endeavoring to consume the reptile.

Moreover, the horned reptile displays a striking skill to shoot blood from the sides of its eyes, arriving at distances of up to five feet. The blood contains a harmful substance that can stop hunters, and the flexibility of this physiological protection adds one more layer to the reptile's self-conservation systems. The joining of mimicry and the capacity to shoot blood features the flexibility of self-preservation components even with different dangers.

In the catlike family, the serval (Leptailurus serval) embodies flexibility in hunting and self-protection systems. The serval has one of a kind actual transformations, including enormous, satellite-dish-like ears that permit it to identify the slightest hints of expected dangers or prey. The flexibility of these particular ears adds to the serval's capacity to identify the development of little well evolved creatures, birds, or bugs in thick grasses.

Moreover, the serval has a noteworthy capacity to jump upward to get airborne prey or explore through tall vegetation. This flexibility in hunting procedures is likewise a self-preservation component, permitting the serval to keep away from possible dangers by quickly jumping to somewhere safe. The mix of sharp tangible transformations and actual readiness features the flexibility of the serval in both hunting and avoiding peril.

In the tremendous spreads of the sea, the versatile self-protection systems of the octopus (Octopoda request) are especially charming. Octopuses are experts of cover, equipped for changing the variety and surface of their skin to match their environmental elements. The versatility of octopus cover fills in as both a method for hunting and a guard against hunters. When compromised, octopuses may utilize problematic examples, for example, intense stripes or emotional variety changes, to surprise or befuddle hunters.

Past disguise, an octopus animal groups show a noteworthy capacity to launch a haze of ink into the water as a bait. The ink cloud makes a distraction, permitting the octopus to escape from hunters. The versatility of these double components — disguise and ink protection — features the refinement of octopus self-preservation methodologies in the dynamic and outwardly complex submerged climate.

In the realm of birds, the hooded pitohui (Pitohui dichrous) in Papua New Guinea addresses a charming instance of synthetic self-preservation. The quills and skin of the hooded pitohui contain intense neurotoxins, making them poisonous to likely hunters. The versatility of this compound safeguard is a type of aposematism, where the brilliantly hued plumage of the pitohui fills in as an advance notice to likely dangers.

The flexibility of substance protections in the hooded pitohui stretches out to its way of behaving, as the bird is known to participate in anting. Anting includes scouring subterranean insects or other poisonous arthropods on the quills, using the synthetic mixtures delivered by these organic entities for extra assurance against ectoparasites. The mix of synthetic protections, aposematism, and anting ways of behaving features the versatility of the hooded pitohui in discouraging hunters and guaranteeing its own security.

In the domain of warm blooded creatures, the versatile self-protection systems of the pangolin (Pholidota request) feature a one of a kind mix of actual transformations and conduct. Pangolins are canvassed in extreme, covering scales made of keratin, shaping a defensive shield. The flexibility of this actual protection lies in the construction of the scales, which are exceptionally successful in safeguarding the pangolin from hunters.

When undermined, pangolins show a way of behaving known as "moving up," where they twist into a tight ball with their scales shaping a defensive obstruction. The versatility of this guarded stance makes it trying for hunters to get to weak body parts. Moreover, some pangolin species have specific organs that can transmit a putrid emission, giving an extra line of protection. The combination of protection, guarded stance, and compound obstacles grandstands the flexibility of pangolins in warding off expected dangers.

The bumble bee (Apis mellifera) embodies the flexibility of self-protection components inside friendly bug states. Bumble bees have an aggregate safeguard technique to safeguard their hive, with working drones displaying both physical and social transformations. The flexibility of bumble bee stinging components includes a changed ovipositor, which can be utilized as a stinger.

At the point when a bumble bee stings, the thorned stinger becomes stopped in the objective, making the honey bee penance its own life. The versatility of this self-conciliatory way of behaving is additionally improved by the arrival of caution pheromones, flagging other working drones to answer forcefully to the apparent danger.

The aggregate guard component of bumble bee states grandstands the flexibility of social bugs in planning both physical and conduct reactions to ultimately benefit the hive.

In the oceanic domain, the pufferfish (Tetraodontidae family) exhibits a momentous self-preservation system including expansion. At the point when undermined, the pufferfish can quickly blow up its body by ingesting water or air, changing into a bigger and seriously testing objective for hunters. The versatility of this actual guard fills in as both a hindrance and a method for safeguarding weak body parts.

Furthermore, some pufferfish species have strong poisons, especially in their inward organs, which can be destructive to hunters whenever ingested. The versatility of synthetic guards adds an additional layer of assurance to the pufferfish's self-safeguarding systems. The coordination of expansion and harmfulness features the flexibility of the pufferfish in discouraging hunters and guaranteeing its own endurance.

In the 8-legged creature world, the vinegaroon (Thelyphonida request) exhibits a fascinating self-protection system including the arrival of a vinegar-like substance. When undermined, vinegaroons can shower acidic corrosive from organs close to the foundation of their whip-like tail, making an obstacle smell. The versatility of this substance protection fills in as an advance notice to possible hunters, making them think long and hard about going after.

The vinegar-like shower isn't just a type of substance protection yet additionally an aggravation that can hinder hunters or expected dangers. The versatility of vinegaroons in using cautious synthetics adds a layer of security to their step by step processes for surviving. This self-preservation system grandstands the versatility of 8-legged creature in utilizing synthetic obstructions to avert dangers.

In the huge and dynamic scenes of the savanna, the versatile self-preservation components of the African cape bison (Syncerus caffer) are especially outstanding. Cape bison are known for their impressive horns, which bend outward and afterward up in an unmistakable shape. The flexibility of these horns lies in their cautious capability, permitting cape bison to avert hunters and potential dangers really.

Cape bison display an aggregate protection technique, frequently framing tight gatherings or "crowds" that act as a unified front against hunters. The versatility of group conduct improves their capacity to distinguish dangers, answer all in all to peril, and use the strength of numbers for assurance. The blend of considerable horns and aggregate protection techniques grandstands the flexibility of cape bison in the difficult conditions they occupy.

3.4: Communication through Claw Use

Correspondence through hook use addresses an entrancing part of creature conduct, displaying the flexibility and versatility of paws past their essential capabilities in hunting, self-preservation, or control of items. Across the animals of the world collectively, different species have developed complex approaches to utilizing hooks as apparatuses for correspondence, permitting them to pass on data, lay out strength, express feelings, and even take part in friendly collaborations. This type of correspondence through paw use features the assorted and refined manners by which living beings have bridled their physical elements to explore the intricacies of their social and biological conditions.

In the avian domain, birds like raptors, hawks, and owls utilize their claws for catching prey as well as for the purpose of correspondence inside their social designs. The flexibility of bird hooks in correspondence is apparent during romance presentations and regional collaborations. Raptors, for instance, utilize their claws to participate in flying presentations, exhibiting their solidarity, nimbleness, and potential as a mate.

During romance presentations, raptors might perform facilitated flights, locking claws mid-air and spiraling towards the ground prior to isolating. This claw locking conduct is a strong type of correspondence, flagging possible mates about their actual ability and similarity for rearing. The flexibility of claws in these flying showcases goes past hunting and stretches out to social cooperations that add to the foundation of reproducing matches.

In regional connections, flying predators might utilize their claws to convey predominance and shield their settling domains. The versatility of claws in these experiences includes visual showcases and actual collaborations where birds utilize their strong hooks to battle off gatecrashers. The correspondence through claw use in these settings lays out and keep up with social pecking orders inside a populace.

In the primate world, explicitly among extraordinary gorillas, for example, chimpanzees and gorillas, correspondence through hook use is seen during social associations and presentations of predominance. While primates don't have paws in similar sense as birds or reptiles, they have altered nails that serve comparative capabilities. Chimpanzees, for example, utilize their long, bended nails for preparing, separating bugs, and participating in friendly prepping ways of behaving.

The versatility of primate hooks in correspondence is obvious in preparing ceremonies, where people utilize their nails to look over the fur of their kindred gathering individuals. Prepping fills clean needs as well as a type of social holding and correspondence.

The demonstration of prepping with hooks conveys trust, collaboration, and social congruity inside the gathering. Moreover, primates might involve their nails for non-forceful material correspondence, tenderly contacting or scratching others to communicate affiliative ways of behaving.

In the reptilian domain, correspondence through paw use is pervasive among different reptile species. A fascinating model is the anole reptile (Anolis spp.), which uses its particular toe cushions and hooks for many-sided shows during social associations. The versatility of anole hooks in correspondence includes both visual and material flagging.

Male anole reptiles take part in intricate regional showcases to lay out strength and draw in mates. The correspondence through hook use incorporates head-bouncing, dewlap augmentations (throat fans), and push-up shows, where the reptile expands its body while showing its dewlap. The utilization of paws becomes an integral factor when the reptile secures itself to a roost and broadens its dewlap utilizing its rear appendages, underlining its size and strength. This visual correspondence through hooks adds to the foundation of regions and mate choice inside anole populaces.

In the catlike family, correspondence through paw use is a conspicuous element among enormous felines like lions and tigers. While hooks in huge felines principally fill hunting and self-preservation needs, they are likewise utilized in friendly collaborations inside a pride or gathering. The flexibility of huge feline paws in correspondence is obvious during showcases of predominance, region checking, and laying out friendly bonds.

Lions, for instance, utilize their paws during showcases of animosity or strength over different individuals from the pride. The demonstration of unsheathing and broadening the paws is a visual sign, showing status for expected struggle or declaring predominance inside the social progressive system. The flexibility of hooks in these collaborations supports the correspondence of economic wellbeing and keeps everything under control inside the pride.

Domain stamping is one more type of correspondence through paw use in huge felines. Lions and other huge felids might scratch tree trunks or the ground with their hooks, making visual and olfactory imprints. The fragrance organs in the paws discharge pheromones, passing on data about the singular's presence, conceptive status, and domain limits. The versatility of paws in this setting goes past actual correspondence to include synthetic flagging, upgrading the viability of checking and correspondence.

In the marine domain, correspondence through paw use is seen among shellfish, especially with regards to mating customs and regional questions. Fiddler crabs (Uca spp.) represent this type of correspondence through the transformation of their augmented paw, which is profoundly deviated in guys. The versatility of fiddler crab paws in correspondence is essential for drawing in mates and laying out regions.

Male fiddler crabs utilize their larger than usual paw in visual presentations during romance customs. The cadenced waving of the huge hook is a visual sign that passes on data about the male's wellbeing, force, and reasonableness as a mate. The versatility of the hook in this setting fills in as an essential method for correspondence in the cutthroat climate of reproducing regions.

Moreover, fiddler crabs utilize their paws in regional debates with adjoining guys. The waving and wielding of the enormous hook act as a visual advance notice to rivals, conveying the singular's readiness to protect its region. The versatility of fiddler crab paws in both romance and regional associations features their multifunctional job in correspondence inside the setting of their complicated social designs.

Correspondence through paw use stretches out to different species, including bugs like insects and honey bees. In insects, specific designs called tarsal hooks are fundamental for route, climbing, and correspondence inside the province. The flexibility of insect hooks in correspondence is seen in different settings, including trail-following, prepping, and animosity.

Insects utilize their hooks to detect compound signals left by different individuals from the settlement, permitting them to follow laid out trails to food sources or explore back to the home. The flexibility of hooks in this setting works with productive correspondence and coordination inside the state. Furthermore, insects might utilize their paws during prepping ways of behaving, where people utilize their mandibles and hooks to clean and eliminate unfamiliar substances from the assortments of nestmates.

In the realm of honey bees, correspondence through paw use is seen during complex ways of behaving, for example, the "waggle dance." Bumble bees (Apis mellifera) utilize this dance to convey the area of food sources to different individuals from the hive. While the essential correspondence happens through body developments and pheromones, the flexibility of honey bee paws is associated with material cooperations during the dance.

During the waggle dance, a forager honey bee getting back to the hive passes on data about the distance and heading of a food source through unambiguous dance designs. Other working drones might connect with the artist, contacting her body with their radio wires and hooks. These material associations upgrade correspondence inside the hive, permitting foragers to assemble data about the area and nature of food sources.

In the domain of birds, parrots feature a fascinating type of correspondence through hook use, especially during social communications and holding ceremonies. Parrots, known for their knowledge and complex social ways of behaving, utilize their paws for roosting and moving as well as for participating in material correspondence with conspecifics and human buddies.

The versatility of parrot hooks in correspondence is clear during affiliative ways of behaving like shared trimming. Parrots utilize their paws to tenderly prepare the quills of their flockmates, supporting social bonds and exhibiting trust and participation. The material idea of this correspondence through hook use encourages a feeling of local area inside the herd, adding to the general union and prosperity of the gathering.

Correspondence through hook use isn't restricted to explicit scientific categorizations; rather, it is a far reaching peculiarity across different environments and developmental heredities. From the amazing claw showcases of raptors to the perplexing paw motioning of scavangers, creatures have developed to use their hooks as adaptable apparatuses for passing on data, laying out friendly designs, and exploring the complicated elements of their surroundings.

Chapter 4

The Science Behind Enormous Talons

The science behind colossal claws dives into the complex life systems, developmental transformations, and biological meaning of these imposing designs across the collective of animals. Claws, described by their sharp and bended nature, are specific hooks that fill different needs, including hunting, self-preservation, and regional showcase. Analyzing the logical parts of gigantic claws gives experiences into the transformative cycles that have formed these designs and their job in the endurance and progress of assorted species.

The life systems of tremendous claws is a result of developmental cycles that have tweaked these designs to meet explicit environmental necessities. Flying predators, like falcons, birds of prey, and owls, display probably the most unmistakable instances of gigantic claws. The science behind these avian claws includes a blend of skeletal transformations, solid designs, and the keratinous covering that frames the hook.

The skeletal design of avian claws is portrayed by the stretching and curve of the terminal phalanges, or bones, in the digits. This variation permits the claws to be lengthened and strongly pointed, making an impressive getting a handle on device. The muscular structure related with claws is profoundly evolved, giving the strength and accuracy expected for catching and quelling prey. The unpredictable interchange among ligaments and muscles empowers flying predators to control the expansion and withdrawal of their claws with exceptional ability.

Moreover, the keratinous covering of claws, like that of nails in people, shapes an extreme and sharp external layer. The keratin sheath safeguards the basic designs and guarantees the strength of the claw during hunting and different exercises. The sythesis and construction of keratin add to the hardness and sharpness of the claw, permitting it to puncture and clutch prey actually.

Colossal claws in flying predators assume a vital part in their hunting techniques. The science behind claw use during predation includes a mix of visual keenness, flight capacities, and the specific transformations of the actual claws. Raptors utilize their sharp visual perception to recognize expected prey from huge spans, and their strong flight permits them to approach and trap targets quickly.

Once in nearness to prey, the colossal claws become possibly the most important factor. The study of claw use during hunting is an exact and facilitated process. Raptors expand their claws in the last snapshots of the assault, guaranteeing that the sharp focuses connect with the prey. The bended idea of the claws works with the hold, keeping the prey from getting away. The strength of the claws, combined with the power produced during the assault, permits raptors to get and convey prey that might try and surpass their own body weight.

Past the avian domain, colossal claws are likewise seen in different earthbound and oceanic species. The science behind claw advancement in these creatures mirrors the assorted environmental specialties and particular tensions that have formed these designs. Among earthbound hunters, enormous cats, for example, lions and tigers, show considerable retractable hooks that are practically like claws.

The life systems of cat paws includes particular sheaths and an instrument that permits the hooks to be expanded and withdrawn. The science behind retractable hooks lies in the flexible tendons and muscles that control the development. Cats utilize their hooks principally for hunting and climbing, displaying the adaptability of these designs in both offense and guard. The retractable idea of the paws helps keep them sharp and limits wear during non-use, featuring the effectiveness of this variation.

In sea-going conditions, the science behind gigantic claws is exemplified by marine hunters like the osprey. The osprey, otherwise called the ocean peddle, has advanced claws adjusted for getting fish.

The one of a kind construction of osprey claws includes reversible external toes, permitting them to get a handle on fish with two claws in front and two behind. This variation empowers ospreys to keep a safe grasp on elusive and wriggling prey while in flight. The osprey's capacity to dive into the water and grab fish with its claws shows the exact coordination and versatility of these designs in oceanic hunting.

The developmental history of huge claws mirrors the specific tensions and environmental difficulties looked by changed species. The science behind claw development includes a complicated transaction of hereditary variety, normal choice, and variation to explicit biological specialties. In the avian domain, the advancement of claws in flying predators is intently attached to their savage way of life and the requirement for proficient prey catch.

The predecessors of present day flying predators probably displayed essential claw structures, and after some time, the development of extended and sharp claws became beneficial for getting a handle on and immobilizing prey. The variation of claws permitted these birds to take advantage of explicit specialties as dominant hunters, where their hunting ability turned into a vital consider their endurance and conceptive achievement.

In the transformative weapons contest among hunters and prey, the science behind claw development is formed by the coevolutionary elements of hunter prey communications. As prey species foster safeguards, like speed, deftness, or defensive covering, hunters, thusly, develop transformations to defeat these protections. Colossal claws address one such transformation that improves the ruthless capacities of specific species.

The study of coevolution is clear in the weapons contest among raptors and their prey. As prey species foster systems to avoid catch, raptors advance more keen, more grounded, and more particular claws to keep up with their effectiveness as trackers. This coevolutionary dance has worked out north of millions of years, bringing about the variety of claw structures saw in various flying predator species.

As well as hunting, tremendous claws likewise act as instruments for self-preservation and regional presentation. The science behind claw use in these settings includes a blend of natural ways of behaving and learned methodologies. Raptors, for instance, may utilize their claws to safeguard themselves against possible dangers, whether from different hunters or from people infringing an on their area.

Regional presentation through claw use is seen in different species, including flying predators and certain reptiles. The science behind this conduct lies in the visual correspondence of strength and regional limits. Raptors might participate in claw shows, where they raise and spread their claws as a visual sign to opponents or gatecrashers. This conduct imparts a status for struggle and builds up the regional limits that are pivotal for getting assets and conceptive achievement.

The versatility of gigantic claws isn't restricted to earthbound conditions. The science behind claws in marine hunters, like the osprey, includes special variations for hunting in oceanic territories. The reversible external toes of the osprey's claws consider a compelling grasp on tricky fish, exhibiting the versatility of these designs to various natural difficulties.

The size and morphology of tremendous claws additionally shift among species, mirroring the particular requests of their environmental jobs. Bigger claws might be invaluable for catching bigger prey, while more modest and more spry claws might be appropriate for hunting more modest or more subtle prey. The science behind claw size and morphology is impacted by variables like eating regimen, natural surroundings, and the particular biological specialty involved by every species.

In the domain of transformative science, the science behind tremendous claws is entwined with the more extensive idea of assembly. Assembly alludes to the free development of comparable qualities in remotely related species because of variation to comparative natural jobs. Colossal claws have developed concurrently in different gatherings, exhibiting the repetitive idea of this transformation in light of the specific tensions of predation and hunting.

For instance, the claws of falcons and those of specific huge felines like cheetahs display concurrent development. While these species have a place with various scientific classifications (birds and well evolved creatures, separately), their claws share practical likenesses because of their common biological job as hunters. The study of union in claw advancement features the repetitive idea of variations that upgrade savage proficiency across assorted ancestries.

The natural meaning of gigantic claws reaches out past the singular organic entity to impact the elements of biological systems. Hunters with compelling claws assume critical parts in forming prey populaces, controlling herbivore numbers, and affecting local area structure. The science behind claws in environmental communications includes a perplexing trap of connections that add to the equilibrium and working of biological systems.

The presence of claw prepared hunters can impact the way of behaving and circulation of prey species. The apprehension about predation by species with colossal claws can prompt changes in prey conduct, for example, modified searching examples, expanded carefulness, or changes in territory use. These conduct reactions have flowing consequences for vegetation, prey networks, and, surprisingly, the elements of hunter prey communications.

Huge claws additionally add to the peculiarity of hierarchical control in environments. The science behind hierarchical control includes the guideline of lower trophic levels by hunters. In environments where claw prepared hunters are available, their hunting exercises can restrict the wealth of herbivores, forestalling overgrazing and advancing the soundness of vegetation. This hierarchical guideline has flowing consequences for the whole environment, impacting the overflow and variety of species at different trophic levels.

The impact of huge claws on environment elements is especially apparent in dominant hunters, which possess the most noteworthy trophic levels. Dominant hunters with compelling claws can serious areas of strength for apply down control, molding the construction and organization of whole biological systems. The science behind the environmental effect of dominant hunters with gigantic claws features their job as cornerstone species, whose presence or nonappearance can significantly affect biodiversity and biological system dependability.

With regards to preservation science, the science behind tremendous claws highlights the significance of safeguarding dominant hunters and their environments. The decay of claw prepared hunters, whether because of natural surroundings misfortune, human-untamed life struggle, or different variables, can have flowing consequences for biological system elements. Preservation endeavors that focus on the insurance of these species add to keeping up with environmental equilibrium and safeguarding the trustworthiness of regular biological systems.

The study of colossal claws additionally converges with concentrates on creature conduct, ethology, and biomechanics. Perceptions of claw use in various species give important experiences into the conduct collection of hunters, their hunting methodologies, and the correspondence components associated with communications with conspecifics. Biomechanical studies investigate the actual properties of claws, like their solidarity, adaptability, and effect force, revealing insight into the mechanical variations that improve their adequacy in predation.

The investigation of claw biomechanics includes tests and examinations to comprehend how claws endure the powers applied during hunting exercises. This exploration adds to how we might interpret the utilitarian morphology of claws and gives experiences into the requirements and variations that shape these designs. Biomechanical reads up likewise have suggestions for fields like advanced mechanics and designing, where analysts look for motivation from nature to plan proficient and flexible holding components.

4.1: Anatomy and Structure of Large Claws

The life systems and design of enormous paws address captivating variations across different species, serving different capabilities like hunting, self-protection, and control of items. Huge hooks have advanced in various taxa, including birds, well evolved creatures, reptiles, and scavangers, displaying the adaptability of this physical element in tending to explicit environmental necessities. Investigating the complex subtleties of the life systems and construction of huge hooks gives experiences into the transformative cycles that have molded these variations and their utilitarian importance in the endurance and progress of organic entities.

In the avian domain, enormous hooks are exemplified by the claws of flying predators, like birds, falcons, and owls. The life systems of avian claws is a noteworthy illustration of developmental specialization for predation. Claws are adjusted hooks tracked down on the toes of raptors, and their design is finely tuned for catching and repressing prey.

The essential parts of avian claws incorporate the terminal phalanges, or bones, of the digits, covered by a keratinous sheath. The terminal phalanges are stretched and bended, framing a sharp point toward the finish of each toe. This transformation permits raptors to get a handle on and immobilize prey during hunting successfully. The ebb and flow of the claws is critical for keeping a protected hold, keeping the prey from getting away once caught.

The keratinous sheath covering the claws is made out of a similar protein tracked down in nails and hooves. This intense external layer safeguards the basic designs and guarantees the solidness of the claw during the afflictions of hunting. The sheath reaches out past the terminal phalanges, shaping a sharp tip that upgrades the ability to penetrate of the claw.

The game plan of claws on the toes is additionally basic to their capability. Raptors regularly have three toes pointing forward and one pointing in reverse, a design known as anisodactyl. The huge, bended claws are situated on the forward-pointing toes, shaping an impressive getting a handle on contraption. This plan permits raptors to seize and clutch prey with accuracy.

The muscle structure related with avian claws is exceptionally evolved, giving the strength and control important for hunting. Ligaments and muscles work in show to control the expansion and withdrawal of the claws, permitting raptors to switch between a resting position and a functioning, hunting stance. The capacity to broaden the claws quickly and with accuracy is vital during the last snapshots of a savage assault.

Notwithstanding flying predators, huge hooks are likewise conspicuous in earthly warm blooded creatures. Among warm blooded animals, the catlike family, including lions, tigers, and cheetahs, exhibits unmistakable variations in the life systems and design of huge hooks. Cat hooks are retractable, an element known as protractile or semi-retractile, permitting them to stay sharp and safeguarded when not being used.

The life systems of cat hooks includes particular sheaths and a component for expansion and withdrawal. The hooks are housed inside the digits, safeguarded by a skin overlap when withdrawn. The capacity to withdraw hooks limits mileage, guaranteeing that the paws stay sharp for hunting and different exercises.

The protractile idea of cat paws is worked with by versatile tendons and muscles that control the development. At the point when a cat broadens its hooks, the tendons and muscles haul the paws out of their defensive sheaths. This component furnishes cats with a viable instrument for hunting, climbing, and self-preservation.

The shape and sharpness of cat paws add to their viability in catching and holding prey. The retractable idea of the hooks permits cats to move toward prey unobtrusively without the unmistakable clicking sound related with broadened paws. This variation upgrades the component of shock during hunting, making cats considerable hunters in different conditions.

In oceanic conditions, the life systems and design of huge paws are seen in marine hunters like scavangers. Shellfish, including crabs, lobsters, and shrimp, display a different exhibit of hook morphologies adjusted to their biological jobs. The life structures of shellfish paws includes jointed sections, chelae (pliers), and specific variations for assorted capabilities.

The jointed sections of scavanger hooks consider a great many developments, giving adaptability and accuracy in catching and controlling items. The chelae, or pliers, shift in size and shape among various species, reflecting transformations to explicit biological specialties. A few shellfish have gigantic, smashing hooks for tearing open shells, while others have thin, apt paws for benefiting from more modest prey or controlling green growth and debris.

The construction of scavanger paws likewise incorporates specific highlights like spines, teeth, and serrations. These transformations improve the effectiveness of the paws in catching and handling food. Scavangers might utilize their hooks for hunting as well as for correspondence, protection, and romance showcases.

The variety of paw structures in shellfish is additionally exemplified by the fiddler crab, an animal groups known for its striking uneven hooks. The significant hook of the male fiddler crab is fundamentally bigger than the minor paw, making an outwardly particular appearance. The life structures of the fiddler crab's paws is adjusted for correspondence and rivalry among guys.

The significant hook of the male fiddler crab is utilized in visual showcases during romance and regional associations. The waving and displaying of the huge hook act as signs to opponents and expected mates. This correspondence through paw shows assumes a vital part in laying out predominance and conceptive accomplishment inside the fiddler crab populace.

In reptiles, the life systems and design of enormous paws are obvious in species like screen reptiles. Screen reptiles are known for their strong appendages and sharp hooks, which they use for climbing, digging, and hunting. The life structures of screen reptile hooks incorporates stretched and bended digits with sharp, pointed tips.

The sharpness of screen reptile hooks is kept up with through regular ways of behaving like scratching and climbing. These exercises assist with eliminating the external layer of the hook, uncovering a new and sharp surface. Screen reptiles utilize their paws for motion as well as for catching and quelling prey.

The flexible idea of enormous hooks is additionally exemplified by the transformation of primates, including lemurs, to explicit biological specialties. Lemurs, found in Madagascar, display a prepping paw, which is a particular variation of the subsequent toe. The prepping paw is prolonged and straightened, working with preparing ways of behaving among people inside gatherings.

The preparing paw of lemurs is utilized for cleaning and keeping up with the fur of themselves and other gathering individuals. This transformation permits lemurs to participate in friendly preparing ways of behaving, supporting social bonds and adding to the general prosperity of the gathering. The construction of the preparing paw mirrors the particular natural and social settings in which lemurs flourish.

4.2: Biological Functions and Adaptations

The natural capabilities and transformations of hooks across different species grandstand the flexibility of this physical component in tending to fundamental parts of endurance, going from hunting and self-protection to preparing and correspondence. Hooks have developed in different taxa, including birds, vertebrates, reptiles, and shellfish, each adjusting to the particular natural specialties and difficulties of their separate surroundings. Investigating the natural capabilities and variations of hooks gives bits of knowledge into the mind boggling manners by which organic entities have saddled this component for their endurance and achievement.

In the avian domain, the natural elements of hooks, explicitly claws, are principal for flying predators, like falcons, birds of prey, and owls. The essential natural capability of avian claws is predation. The sharp, bended construction of claws, combined with the strength and accuracy of the related muscle structure, makes them impressive devices for catching and immobilizing prey.

The transformation of claws for predation includes the development of lengthened and pointed terminal phalanges, covered by an extreme keratinous sheath.

This foundational layout permits raptors to expand their claws quickly and with accuracy during the last snapshots of a savage assault. The organic capability of claws in hunting is exemplified by the capacity of raptors to get and convey prey that might try and surpass their own body weight.

Past hunting, claws serve extra natural capabilities in the domain of self-preservation. Raptors might utilize their claws to avoid possible dangers, whether from different hunters or from people infringing an on their area. The demonstration of unsheathing and shaking claws fills in as a visual advance notice, conveying the preparation for struggle and laying out limits inside their regional space.

The flexibility of avian claws stretches out to correspondence and romance presentations. In certain species, claw locking shows during romance ceremonies exhibit the strength and similarity of possible mates. The visual correspondence through claw shows adds to the foundation of reproducing matches, underscoring the multifunctional job of claws past predation.

In earthbound well evolved creatures, the organic elements of paws are different and custom-made to explicit environmental jobs. The retractable hooks of cats, including lions, tigers, and cheetahs, epitomize a complex transformation for hunting and self-protection. The organic capability of retractable hooks lies in limiting wear and keeping up with sharpness, permitting cats to move toward prey quietly and effectively.

The retractable idea of cat paws likewise serves an organic capability in climbing. Felines utilize their paws for climbing trees, scaling surfaces, and exploring different landscapes. The capacity to withdraw paws when not being used keeps them from getting found out or dulled during non-locomotor exercises.

Notwithstanding predation and climbing, the organic elements of cat paws reach out to correspondence and regional stamping. Scratching surfaces with paws makes visual and olfactory imprints, permitting felines to lay out domain limits and speak with conspecifics. The demonstration of scratching fills in as a multi-layered conduct with both useful and open importance.

Among primates, the organic elements of paws are exemplified by preparing hooks tracked down in lemurs. The stretched and straightened prepping paw, ordinarily on the subsequent toe, serves a particular capability in keeping up with cleanliness inside gatherings. Lemurs utilize their preparing paws for cleaning and eliminating parasites from their fur, as well as participating in friendly prepping ways of behaving with other gathering individuals.

The natural capability of the prepping hook adds to social holding and participation inside lemur gatherings. The versatility of this hook features how an apparently specific element can assume a pivotal part in the social elements and prosperity of an animal types.

In reptiles, especially screen reptiles, hooks serve fundamental natural capabilities connected with hunting and motion. The sharp hooks of screen reptiles are adjusted for catching and repressing prey, including little warm blooded creatures, bugs, and different reptiles. The construction of screen reptile paws incorporates prolonged and pointed digits, considering viable prey catch.

Natural transformations in reptilian hooks are likewise clear with regards to climbing and digging. Screen reptiles utilize their paws for climbing trees, rocks, and different surfaces, displaying the flexibility of these designs in tending to assorted environmental difficulties.

The capacity to dig with paws is fundamental for home development, cover creation, and getting to underground prey.

Shellfish, like crabs and lobsters, show many organic capabilities and transformations in their hooks, known as chelae. The size, shape, and construction of shellfish paws shift among species, reflecting transformations to explicit natural jobs. The natural elements of scavanger paws include hunting, taking care of, protection, and correspondence.

Scavanger paws might be adjusted for squashing, cutting, or getting a handle on, contingent upon the species' eating routine and biological specialty. The construction of shellfish paws incorporates particular highlights like spines, teeth, and serrations, upgrading their effectiveness in catching and handling food. The flexibility of scavanger hooks is obvious in the assorted morphologies saw among various species.

The natural elements of scavanger hooks reach out past predation to correspondence and contest. In fiddler crabs, the uneven hooks of guys serve an open capability during romance and regional collaborations. The waving and wielding of the huge hook add to visual presentations that convey strength and regenerative wellness.

In the marine domain, the organic elements of hooks are exemplified by the osprey's variations for piscivorous hunting. The reversible external toes of the osprey's claws take into consideration a successful grasp on dangerous fish. The versatility of osprey claws exhibits how organic highlights can be finely tuned to the particular difficulties of catching sea-going prey.

Bugs, like subterranean insects and honey bees, additionally display particular natural capabilities in their hooks. Subterranean insects, for instance, utilize their hooks for route, climbing, and correspondence inside the province. The flexibility of insect paws in trail-following and preparing ways of behaving adds to the effectiveness of undertakings inside the social design.

The natural elements of honey bee hooks are obvious in mind boggling ways of behaving, for example, the "waggle dance." Bumble bees utilize their paws for material cooperations during the dance, passing data about the area of food sources on to other hive individuals. The flexibility of honey bee hooks in correspondence grandstands the significance of this physical component in complex social ways of behaving.

Organic variations of hooks are profoundly interwoven with the environmental jobs and specific tensions experienced by various species. The variety of hook designs and works mirrors the developmental reactions to explicit natural difficulties, including predation, headway, correspondence, and social associations.

The flexibility of hooks is additionally featured by joined advancement, where comparative paw structures have developed autonomously in remotely related species confronting comparative environmental requests. This peculiarity highlights the useful meaning of hooks and their repetitive development as answers for normal difficulties in various ancestries.

4.3: Genetic Influences on Claw Development

Hereditary impacts assume a critical part in the improvement of paws across different species, molding the morphology, construction, and elements of these fundamental physical highlights. The hereditary reason for paw improvement is profoundly entwined with the more extensive cycles of development, variation, and the legacy of attributes that give benefits in unambiguous environmental specialties. Analyzing the hereditary impacts on paw improvement gives bits of knowledge into the multifaceted components that oversee the variety and versatility of hooks in the collective of animals.

The improvement of paws is organized by a progression of hereditary cycles that unfurl during undeveloped turn of events. The hereditary outline for paw improvement is encoded in the DNA of a creature, directing the development of tissues, skeletal components, and different designs that add to the last morphology of hooks. The actuation and guideline of explicit qualities guide the complex cell and atomic occasions that shape hooks in various species.

In flying predators, like falcons, birds of prey, and owls, the hereditary impacts on claw improvement are essential for the procurement of specific hunting devices. The hereditary directions encoded in the avian genome guide the arrangement of lengthened and bended terminal phalanges, which are principal to the construction of claws. The outflow of qualities engaged with bone turn of events, like those connected with phalanx prolongation and bend, adds to the extraordinary morphology of avian claws.

The hereditary effects on claw improvement reach out to the guideline of keratin creation. Keratin is the protein that frames the external sheath of claws, giving sturdiness and assurance. Qualities liable for keratin blend are enacted during paw improvement, guaranteeing the development of a tough external layer that upgrades the usefulness and life span of claws.

The hereditary reason for claw improvement is dependent upon normal choice, driving the development of particular transformations in various flying predator species. Transformations or varieties in key qualities related with paw improvement might present benefits in unambiguous natural settings. For instance, a hereditary variety that improves the strength or sharpness of claws might be leaned toward in species that depend vigorously on chasing after their endurance.

The hereditary effects on paw advancement are likewise clear in earthly vertebrates, especially in the catlike family. The retractable hooks of cats, including lions, tigers, and cheetahs, are a consequence of mind boggling hereditary cycles that oversee the improvement of specific muscular build and connective tissues. Qualities related with the protraction and withdrawal of paws assume a significant part in molding the practical parts of cat hooks.

The development of retractable paws in cats is driven by hereditary varieties that present benefits in both hunting and climbing. The capacity to withdraw hooks limits wear and saves them sharp for effective prey catch. Qualities engaged with the improvement of the retractable system are dependent upon particular tensions, inclining toward varieties that upgrade the readiness and covertness of cats during predation.

In scavangers, for example, crabs and lobsters, the hereditary impacts on hook improvement are different, mirroring the heap variations in chelae morphology. Qualities related with appendage improvement, division, and member specialization add to the development of assorted paw structures in scavangers. The initiation of explicit hereditary pathways directs the development and separation of tissues, prompting the improvement of hooks adjusted for different capabilities.

Hereditary effects on shellfish hook improvement are dependent upon natural and environmental elements. Variety in hereditary pathways might lead to various hook morphologies, permitting scavangers to take advantage of explicit specialties and biological jobs. Regular choice follows up on these hereditary varieties, molding the variety of hook structures saw in scavangers across various species and conditions.

The hereditary effects on paw advancement in reptiles, like screen reptiles, add to the arrangement of hooks adjusted for hunting, climbing, and digging. Qualities related with appendage improvement and skeletal development assume basic parts in forming the design and capability of reptilian hooks. The enactment of hereditary pathways during early stage improvement directs the length, curve, and sharpness of hooks in these species.

The versatility of reptilian hooks is reflected in the hereditary varieties that bring about various paw morphologies. Species occupying assorted conditions might show hereditary variations that upgrade their capacity to flourish in unambiguous natural specialties. For instance, the hereditary effects on hook advancement in arboreal species might lean toward longer and more bended paws, working with climbing and getting a handle on.

In lemurs, the hereditary effects on preparing hook improvement highlight the particular transformations that add to social ways of behaving and overall vibes. Qualities engaged with appendage improvement and digit separation guide the arrangement of the preparing paw, which is prolonged and leveled. The hereditary reason for the prepping paw is custom fitted to the particular natural and social settings wherein lemurs live.

Hereditary effects on paw improvement stretch out to the atomic level, where the guideline of quality articulation and the associations between flagging pathways assume vital parts. The actuation or restraint of explicit qualities at various transformative phases decides the exact attributes of paws, including size, shape, and usefulness. Sub-atomic components, for example, quality guideline, cell flagging, and tissue separation are organized by the hereditary code encoded in a living being's DNA.

The transformative history of paws is formed by hereditary changes that collect over ages. The course of regular determination follows up on hereditary varieties, leaning toward characteristics that improve the wellness and endurance of people in unambiguous conditions. Hereditary transformations in paw improvement add to the variety of hook structures saw in various species, mirroring the powerful exchange between hereditary impacts and biological tensions.

United development, where comparable paw structures advance freely in remotely related species, features the repetitive idea of hereditary variations because of normal biological difficulties. The hereditary effects on hook advancement unite to deliver practically equivalent to structures that serve comparative capabilities in various genealogies. This peculiarity highlights the flexibility and adaptability of hereditary cycles in molding the development of paws.

The hereditary effects on hook advancement are not static however dependent upon progressing transformative cycles. Hereditary varieties emerge through systems like transformation, recombination, and quality stream, adding to the variety of hook structures inside populaces. Over the long run, hereditary transformations that present benefits in unambiguous biological settings might become predominant through normal choice, affecting the general direction of paw advancement.

Bugs, like subterranean insects and honey bees, additionally display hereditary effects on hook advancement, especially with regards to particular ways of behaving. Qualities related with appendage improvement and member morphology guide the arrangement of paws in bugs, adding to their different capabilities. The hereditary effects on hook advancement in bugs are custom-made to explicit ways of behaving like digging, climbing, and getting a handle on.

The hereditary reason for paw advancement in bugs is unpredictably connected to their biological jobs and social ways of behaving. In subterranean insect provinces, for instance, the hereditary effects on hook advancement add to the proficiency of errands like scrounging, home development, and prepping. The flexibility of bug paws mirrors the powerful interchange between hereditary varieties and the environmental difficulties looked by these species.

The hereditary effects on paw improvement have more extensive ramifications for grasping the developmental elements of member variety in the collective of animals. Paws address a momentous illustration of how hereditary variations add to the practical variety of designs that are fundamental for endurance, predation, correspondence, and social collaborations.

The investigation of hereditary effects on hook improvement gives a window into the fundamental instruments that shape the fantastic assortment of paws saw across various taxa.

4.4: Comparative Studies across Species

Relative investigations across species give an important structure to grasping the variety and development of hooks, uncovering shared designs, interesting transformations, and the biological meaning of this flexible physical element. Looking at hooks across changed taxa, including birds, well evolved creatures, reptiles, and shellfish, permits us to disentangle the shared traits and varieties in design, capability, and conduct related with these particular limbs.

In the avian realm, paws, known as claws in flying predators, are unmistakable elements that have developed for effective predation. Relative examinations across avian species uncover shared qualities in claw design and capability. The presence of stretched and bended terminal phalanges, covered by a keratinous sheath, is a typical topic. This underlying combination features the versatile meaning of claws in getting a handle on, holding, and immobilizing prey during hunting.

Similar examinations likewise grandstand varieties in claw morphology among various flying predator species. Bigger species, like hawks, may have vigorous and strong claws adjusted for catching bigger prey, while more modest raptors, similar to kestrels, may have more lithe claws appropriate for hunting more modest or tricky prey. These varieties reflect variations to various natural specialties and prey types inside the avian request.

Past primary angles, similar investigations of claws uncover varieties in hunting ways of behaving. Raptors utilize a blend of flying moves, visual keenness, and the exact utilization of claws during savage strikes. Peregrine hawks, for instance, are known for their rapid aeronautical jumps, using claws with astounding accuracy to catch birds mid-flight. Conversely, owls, with their nighttime way of life, utilize quiet flight and strong claws to catch prey in low-light circumstances.

Relative examinations across avian species additionally feature the job of claws in regional safeguard and romance showcases. Raptors frequently participate in claw locking shows, exhibiting the strength and similarity of likely mates or conveying predominance in regional connections. The adaptability of claws in both hunting and social ways of behaving highlights their importance in the avian world.

In the earthly warm blooded creature class, relative investigations of paws give bits of knowledge into the different variations for predation, climbing, self-preservation, and other biological jobs. Cat hooks, portrayed by their retractable nature, are a subject of interest in relative examinations.

The capacity to withdraw paws limits wear, permitting them to stay sharp for hunting, climbing, and different exercises. Lions, tigers, and cheetahs display varieties in hook size and construction, reflecting variations to various hunting systems and conditions.

Similar examinations likewise uncover concurrent development in the retractable paw system. The two felines and certain individuals from the mongoose family, like genets, have autonomously developed retractable hooks. This combination in hook variations highlights the particular benefits of such designs in ruthless ways of life, where exact and controlled paw use is fundamental for progress.

As opposed to the retractable hooks of felids, canids, like wolves and homegrown canines, have non-retractable paws. Similar examinations enlighten the utilitarian distinctions among retractable and non-retractable paws, with the last option serving different jobs in digging, footing, and solidness during running. The variety of paw transformations in well evolved creatures mirrors the biological specialties and ways of life of various species.

Primates, including lemurs, show interesting paw transformations that add to their arboreal ways of life. Lemurs have specific prepping hooks, especially on the subsequent toe, which are prolonged and smoothed. Near examinations across primates uncover varieties in preparing hook size and morphology, reflecting variations to explicit environmental and social settings. Prepping paws work with social associations, upkeep of fur cleanliness, and add to the perplexing social elements inside lemur gatherings.

In reptiles, near examinations across species feature the variety of hook transformations for movement, hunting, and digging. Screen reptiles, known for their strong appendages and sharp paws, are subjects of interest in such examinations. The lengthened and pointed digits of screen reptile hooks add to successful prey catch and climbing. Near examinations uncover varieties in paw size and arch among various screen reptile species, reflecting variations to assorted environments and prey types.

Near examinations likewise stretch out to scavangers, where chelae, or hooks, show exceptional variety in structure and capability. Crabs, lobsters, and shrimp exhibit varieties in hook morphology adjusted to various natural jobs. The devastating hooks of crabs, for example, are appropriate for tearing open shells and catching prey. Similar examinations uncover transformations in chelae structure, including specific highlights like spines, teeth, and serrations, upgrading the proficiency of hooks for different capabilities.

The fiddler crab, a novel model in shellfish, displays articulated sexual dimorphism in hook size. Relative examinations across fiddler crab species uncover varieties in the size and morphology of the significant paw, which is fundamentally bigger in guys. This sexual dimorphism is related with romance presentations and regional associations, featuring the job of paws in conceptive ways of behaving.

Bugs, with their assorted transformations, additionally add to similar investigations of hooks. Insects, honey bees, and different arthropods have particular hooks that work with exercises like climbing, digging, and getting a handle on. Similar examinations uncover varieties in paw morphology among various bug species, reflecting transformations to their environmental jobs inside settlements or natural surroundings.

Near examinations across species enlighten united advancement, where comparable hook structures have freely developed in remotely related genealogies. The peculiarity of united advancement highlights the practical meaning of hooks in tending to normal environmental difficulties. For example, the merged development of retractable paws in the two felines and certain mongoose species features the specific benefits of this transformation in ruthless ways of life.

The biological meaning of hooks is a focal subject in relative examinations, uncovering the manners by which various species have adjusted paws to their particular environments, diets, and ways of life. The flexibility of hooks in tending to a scope of capabilities, from predation and movement to preparing and social cooperations, highlights their versatile worth in different biological settings.

Similar examinations likewise add to how we might interpret developmental cycles, exhibiting the unique exchange between hereditary impacts and natural tensions. The varieties and unions saw in hook transformations across species give significant experiences into the particular tensions that have formed the variety of paw structures throughout developmental time.

Chapter 5

Tales of Terrifying Encounters

Stories of startling experiences with imposing animals having threatening hooks have been woven into the texture of human legends and folklore, rising above societies and civic establishments. These stories, went down through ages, act as preventative accounts, impressions of base feelings of trepidation, and illustrations for the secrets and risks of the regular world. From the legendary monsters of antiquated legends to cryptids and puzzling animals that torment contemporary minds, the subject of startling experiences with mauled elements continues, taking advantage of the profound openings of the human mind.

In old folklore, various societies across the globe have made stories of huge animals with fearsome hooks, typifying the more obscure parts of the regular world. One such model is the Fabrication, an animal from Greek folklore, portrayed as a half and half monster with the body of a lion, the top of a goat emerging from its back, and a snake for a tail. This diverse animal's hooks were supposed to be basically as sharp as edges, striking fear into the hearts of the people who thought for even a moment to confront it. The Fabrication filled in as an image of disorder, a power that couldn't be quickly restrained or prevailed.

In Norse folklore, the fearsome mythical serpent Níðhöggr, living underneath the underlying foundations of Yggdrasil, the World Tree, was said to have dangerously sharp hooks. This massive snake, with its paws continually bothering the foundations of the World Tree, addressed the horrendous powers that undermined the soundness of the universe. Stories of Níðhöggr's frightening presence filled in as a sign of the tricky harmony among request and confusion in the Norse cosmology.

Asian old stories is rich with stories of legendary animals, and the Chinese folklore presents the fearsome Taotie, a twisted animal frequently portrayed with sharp paws and an insatiable craving. The Taotie is known for gobbling up everything in its way, representing voracious eagerness and ravenousness. The animal's threatening hooks become representations for the damaging outcomes of uncontrolled longings, advance notice against the dangers of extravagance and overabundance.

Moving past old folklores, contemporary stories of cryptids and incredible animals keep on dazzling minds with records of alarming experiences. One such model is the unbelievable Chupacabra, a cryptid starting in Latin American fables yet earning worldwide respect. Depicted as an animal looking like a reptilian kangaroo with sharp paws and an inclination for going after domesticated animals, the Chupacabra has turned into an image of country fears and the unexplored world. Stories of experiences with the Chupacabra add to a cutting edge legends that mixes components of secret, repulsiveness, and the unexplained.

The Wendigo, a legendary animal from Algonquian fables, is one more model that exemplifies the dread of mauled experiences. Portrayed as a noxious, extraordinary being with a voracious craving for human tissue, the Wendigo is frequently portrayed with extended appendages and dangerously sharp hooks. Accounts of the Wendigo are established in the social feelings of dread of starvation, savagery, and the cruel real factors of endurance in the unforgiving wild.

The domain of cryptozoology, which investigates the presence of animals outside the extent of standard science, presents stories of frightening experiences with obscure elements. The notorious Mothman, a cryptid related with the Point Charming region in West Virginia, is many times depicted as a humanoid figure with huge wings and sparkling red eyes. A few records incorporate notices of sharp paws, adding an additional layer of repulsiveness to the strange sightings. The Mothman's standing as a harbinger of catastrophe and destruction has woven its direction into the legends of the locale, turning into an image of looming disaster.

In the records of present day ghastliness fiction, the werewolf, an animal with a double nature of man and wolf, frequently portrayed with sharp hooks during its change, keeps on being a staple of startling experiences. The thought of a human capitulating to a basic, brutish nature affected by the full moon resounds with well established fears of letting completely go and the eccentric dimness inside.

Stories of werewolf experiences, whether established in fables or investigated in writing and film, exploit the mental dread of losing one's humankind to the wild impulses epitomized by well honed hooks.

Cryptids like the Jersey Fallen angel, said to possess the Pine Barrens of New Jersey, additionally add to the woven artwork of alarming experiences. Portrayals of the Jersey Villain frequently incorporate elements, for example, weathered wings, a pony like head, and, remarkably, sharp paws. Sightings and accounts of the Jersey Fiend, going back hundreds of years, feed into the old stories of the locale, where the animal is accepted to bring incident and catastrophe.

The appeal of stories highlighting frightening ripped at experiences stretches out to artistic and abstract domains, where animals of bad dreams become completely awake. One notable model is the Xenomorph from the "Outsider" film establishment. This extraterrestrial species, known for its acidic blood and stretched, dangerously sharp paws, typifies the base feeling of dread toward an obscure and exceptionally deadly foe. The Xenomorph's capacity to involve its hooks for both predation and self-preservation adds layers of strain to the account, intensifying the ghastliness of extraterrestrial experiences.

In the loathsomeness classification, the idea of the Wendigo has been rethought in different structures, adding to a tradition of startling experiences in writing and film. The Wendigo's presence, frequently joined by its threatening paws, represents the more obscure parts of human instinct, investigating subjects of barbarianism, confinement, and the powerful results of untouchable activities. Such stories tap into mental ghastliness, where the paws of the Wendigo act as representations for the inevitable results of surrendering to base, prohibited wants.

The getting through interest with stories of startling ripped at experiences additionally reaches out to metropolitan legends and contemporary fables. Accounts of animals sneaking in the shadows, equipped with dangerously sharp paws and a preference for the obscure, persevere in our aggregate creative mind. These stories, whether shared around pit fires, talked about in quieted tones, or sensationalized in media, play upon the widespread anxiety toward the concealed and the untamed.

Experiences with cryptids like the Goatman, an animal reputed to have goat-like elements and sharp paws, have turned into the stuff of present day legends. Likewise with numerous cryptids, the Goatman's starting points are covered in secret, with stories circling in different locales. The equivocalness encompassing these animals and their ripped at experiences uplifts the tension and interest, encouraging a feeling of marvel and dread in the people who hear these stories.

In the computerized age, where stories can be shared worldwide with the snap of a button, stories of frightening experiences with ripped at substances track down new life on web gatherings, virtual entertainment, and online networks committed to the paranormal.

Records of claimed cryptid sightings, secretive animals sneaking in the wild, or unexplained hook stamps abandoned become piece of a virtual fables that obscures the lines among truth and fiction.

The mental effect of stories highlighting unnerving ripped at experiences is established in the base anxiety toward the obscure and the instinctual consciousness of the perils that prowl in the wild. Whether grounded in antiquated folklores, territorial fables, or contemporary metropolitan legends, these stories tap into general feelings of dread that rise above social limits. The imagery of hooks as instruments of predation, risk, and the untamed powers of nature resounds with the human mind, conjuring an instinctive reaction that rises above levelheadedness.

As we dive into these stories of frightening experiences with ripped at elements, we explore the domain where reality and creative mind obscure, where the obscure turns into the wellspring of both interest and dread. These accounts, went down through ages or arising in the advanced age, mirror mankind's getting through interest with the secrets of the regular world and the animals that occupy the shadows.

Whether confronting legendary monsters, cryptids, or animals from the profundities of fables, the subject of frightening experiences with paws stays a strong story component that proceeds to enamor and torment the human creative mind.

5.1: Mythology and Folklore Surrounding Claws

Folklore and legends from societies all over the planet are saturated with stories that element paws as images, devices, or characteristics of legendary creatures, animals, and gods. The meaning of paws in folklore goes past their actual capability, diving into the domains of imagery, power, and the timeless battle among great and malevolence. From old civic establishments to contemporary societies, the stories encompassing hooks offer a rich embroidery of implying that mirrors humankind's intricate relationship with the regular world and the strange powers that shape our convictions.

In different folklores, paws frequently highlight unmistakably as characteristics of strong and frequently tremendous creatures. The Delusion, an animal from Greek folklore, is one such model. This fearsome crossover had the body of a lion, the top of a goat projecting from its back, and a snake for a tail — all components adding to a considerable and twisted picture. The lion's paws, sharp and lethal, became representative of the Fabrication's fierceness and its ability for obliteration. The legend of the Delusion, with its unnerving paws, fills in as a useful example about the results of untamed and turbulent powers.

In Norse folklore, the enormous wolf Fenrir epitomizes the duality of force and peril related with paws. Fenrir, bound to assume a crucial part in the prophetically calamitous occasions of Ragnarok, was said to have jaws that could consume the sun and the moon.

His considerable hooks, alongside his unquenchable hunger, made him an image of mayhem and obliteration. The Norse pantheon perceived the tremendous power and danger presented by Fenrir's hooks, meshing them into predictions of a calamitous finish to the world.

Paws are frequently connected with heavenly or extraordinary creatures, representing both security and threat. In old Egyptian folklore, the goddess Sekhmet is portrayed with lioness highlights, including sharp paws, underscoring her job as a savage defender. Sekhmet's paws, seen as instruments of heavenly equity, were accepted to avoid evil and keep vast control. This duality — hooks as both defensive and damaging — mirrors the perplexing idea of divinities in fanciful customs.

Moving toward the east, Chinese folklore presents the fearsome Nian, a legendary monster related with the lunar new year. As indicated by legend, the Nian had sharp paws and tusks and would threaten towns. Be that as it may, the animal was at last impeded by the utilization of boisterous commotions and red. The Nian's paws became images of the difficulties looked by networks, and the legends encompassing its loss conveyed the force of solidarity and creativity in conquering misfortune.

In Hindu folklore, the goddess Durga is frequently portrayed with numerous arms, each using a weapon, including hooks or nails. Durga's ten arms address her imposing power, and her paws represent her capacity to overcome insidious powers. The picture of Durga with her hooks took part fighting against devils highlights the topic of help from above and the victory of good over evil.

The emblematic meaning of paws isn't restricted to animals or gods; it reaches out to amazing legends too. The Greek legend Perseus, known for killing the Gorgon Medusa, is much of the time portrayed employing a sickle-molded blade, underlining the significance of accuracy and the intensity of a very much pointed strike. The association between Perseus' weapon and the idea of hooks features the emblematic power credited to sharp, cutting executes in legendary accounts.

In Local American folklore, the Thunderbird is a strong and grand animal frequently connected with tempests and lightning. With claws equipped for holding thunderclaps, the Thunderbird represents both the damaging power of nature and the extraordinary force of tempests. The Thunderbird's hooks, portrayed as imposing weapons, encapsulate the crude basic energy tackled by this legendary being.

Legendary animals with hooks are not restricted to antiquated developments; they continue in the old stories of later societies. In the fables of the native people groups of North America, the Wendigo is a startling animal related with winter, starvation, and barbarianism.

Depicted as having lengthened appendages and extremely sharp hooks, the Wendigo encapsulates the base apprehensions of starvation and the risks of surrendering to taboo longings. The paws of the Wendigo act as the two apparatuses of predation and images of the results of no activities.

Asian legends presents the Nue, an animal from Japanese folklore with the top of a monkey, the body of a raccoon canine, the legs of a tiger, and a snake for a tail. The Nue's sharp hooks, alongside its cross breed highlights, inspire a feeling of otherworldly risk. As indicated by legend, the Nue was crushed by the legend Minamoto no Yorimasa, featuring the emblematic victory of human mental fortitude over heavenly dangers.

The imagery of hooks reaches out past fanciful animals to shape social convictions and ceremonies. In a few African societies, creature paws are accepted to have profound importance and are utilized in ceremonies to conjure the defensive characteristics of the creatures from which they start. The paws are viewed as conductors for the embodiment and force of the creatures, interfacing people to the profound domain.

The idea of shape-moving creatures, frequently furnished with hooks, is common in world folklore. In Local American legends, the skinwalker is a powerful being with the capacity to change into different creatures, once in a while highlighting sharp paws or claws. These creatures are frequently connected with perniciousness and are accepted to have dim abilities. The presence of hooks in their changed states fills in as a visual portrayal of the extraordinary and the uncanny.

Legendary accounts frequently use paws as allegories for base senses, untamed powers of nature, and the battle among request and tumult. In Slavic legends, the Zmey Gorynych is a winged serpent with different heads, each bearing sharp teeth and hooks. The legend Dobrynya Nikitich, who faces the mythical serpent in fight, exemplifies the human battle against immense, tumultuous powers. The Zmey Gorynych's hooks address the disastrous idea of the winged serpent, and the legend's triumph represents the victory of request and mental fortitude.

The imagery of hooks likewise stretches out to animals that ride the limit between the legendary and the genuine. In Scottish old stories, the kelpie is a water soul that can change into a pony and, in certain varieties, has webbed hooks rather than hooves. The kelpie's paws, related with its sea-going nature, represent the baffling and flighty parts of waterways. Stories of experiences with the kelpie act as alerts about the risks prowling in lakes and streams.

Contemporary mainstream society keeps on drawing motivation from fanciful and folkloric themes, making new stories that highlight animals with hooks. In the domain of imagination writing and gaming, mythical serpents with sharp hooks, as Smaug from J.R.R. Tolkien's "The Hobbit," epitomize the model of the tremendous, treasure-protecting snake.

These cutting edge translations keep up with the emblematic connection among paws and the basic, untamed powers of legendary creatures.

The persevering through interest with hooks in folklore and legends addresses their representative reverberation and the widespread topics they epitomize. Hooks, whether employed by divinities, legendary animals, or amazing legends, address the crossing point of force, risk, and the timeless battle among request and turmoil. These stories act as social mirrors, mirroring mankind's endeavors to get a handle on the secrets of the normal world, the obscure, and the powers that shape our aggregate creative mind. The imagery of paws perseveres, associating antiquated legends to contemporary stories, and helping us to remember the ageless power implanted in the prototype picture of sharp, imposing claws.

5.2: Real-life Animal Attacks and Escapes

Genuine creature assaults and escapes have caught the aggregate creative mind for their theatrics, power, and the crude force of the regular world. These episodes, frequently filled by endurance senses, regional debates, or unintentional experiences among people and natural life, act as distinct tokens of the flighty and now and again perilous collaborations that can happen between species. From the heart-halting snapshots of a startling a showdown to the holding accounts of trying getaways, these genuine stories offer a brief look into the intricate elements among people and the untamed occupants of nature.

In the domain of creature assaults, experiences with dominant hunters have been the focal point of various chilling stories. The sheer power and savage senses of animals like lions, tigers, and bears can bring about dangerous circumstances, particularly when the limits between their natural surroundings and human settlements cross-over. Such episodes frequently feature the fragile harmony between protecting regular biological systems and limiting the dangers presented to human populaces.

One striking model is the narrative of Timothy Treadwell, an energetic natural life devotee who lived among mountain bears in Gold country. Treadwell's connections with the bears, recorded in the film "Grizzly Man," eventually prompted a lethal experience in 2003. Notwithstanding Treadwell's profound association with the bears and his central goal to safeguard them, the limits among a wild and human area obscured, bringing about an unfortunate episode that highlighted the intrinsic risks of closeness to dominant hunters.

Additionally, huge feline assaults, especially those including lions and tigers, certainly stand out because of their savagery and the results of imprisonment. Episodes in confidential zoos or offices where extraordinary creatures are kept have prompted dangerous circumstances. The departure of a tiger from the San Francisco Zoo in 2007, bringing about a deadly assault on a guest, brought up issues about the security conventions set up and the moral contemplations of keeping such strong animals in bondage.

Get away, whether coordinated by creatures in bondage or happening in the wild, give enthralling stories of strength and versatility. The tale of Inky, an octopus at the Public Aquarium of New Zealand, acquired global consideration when the smart cephalopod figured out how to get away from its nook and advance toward opportunity in the Pacific Sea. Inky's getaway exhibited the knowledge and critical abilities to think of octopuses, leaving aquarium staff both intrigued and with a recently discovered regard for the animal's impulses.

In a more surprising setting, the 2011 episode including many colorful creatures in Zanesville, Ohio, stunned people in general as news broke of lions, tigers, bears, and different creatures being released by their proprietor before he ended his own life. The resulting tumult incited policing settle on the hard decision to euthanize a large number of the got away from creatures to safeguard public security. The episode focused on the absence of guidelines encompassing the confidential responsibility for creatures and the potential dangers related with their departure.

Gets away from in the wild, frequently including huge hunters, exhibit the versatility and flexibility of these animals even with human-affected conditions. Occurrences of enormous felines, like mountain lions or panthers, wandering into metropolitan regions looking for food or domain have become more successive as human improvement infringes on regular living spaces. These experiences feature the difficulties of conjunction and the significance of preservation endeavors to relieve clashes among natural life and human networks.

In the marine domain, experiences with sharks have powered both trepidation and interest. While shark assaults are genuinely intriguing, they catch public consideration because of the basic apprehension related with these dominant hunters. The narrative of Bethany Hamilton, an expert surfer who lost her arm in a shark assault off the shoreline of Hawaii, turned into a helpful story of flexibility and assurance. Hamilton's re-visitation of cutthroat riding after the assault displayed the human ability to beat difficulty and dread.

On the other side, accounts of creatures getting away from human control, especially in the domain of bazaars and diversion, have revealed insight into the moral worries encompassing the utilization of wild creatures for public entertainment. The tale of Kid, an African elephant who got away from a bazaar in Honolulu in 1994, brought about a grievous showdown with policing, the physical and mental cost for creatures exposed to an existence of imprisonment and execution.

With regards to zoo get away, the 2016 occurrence at the Cincinnati Zoo brought worldwide consideration when a young man fell into the nook of Harambe, a silverback gorilla. The grievous occasion prompted the zoo's choice to euthanize Harambe to guarantee the security of the kid. The occurrence ignited banters about zoo wellbeing measures, parental obligation, and the moral contemplations of keeping creatures in bondage.

While getaways and assaults including huge and magnetic creatures frequently overwhelm titles, more modest animals can likewise present dangers, particularly in locales with different and possibly risky untamed life. Experiences with venomous snakes, bugs, or other little yet powerful creatures can prompt hazardous circumstances, underlining the requirement for mindfulness and training in regions where people and untamed life coincide.

The elements of creature assaults and escapes frequently bring up moral issues about the treatment and the executives of wild and extraordinary creatures. The obligation of people to save regular natural surroundings, execute viable security gauges, and consider the government assistance of creatures in bondage becomes pivotal in moderating expected clashes and guaranteeing the prosperity of the two people and untamed life.

In certain occurrences, the lines between deliberate assaults, protective ways of behaving, and mishaps become obscured. Creatures might see people as dangers to their region or posterity, prompting guarded activities that outcome in assaults. Alternately, human exercises, like infringement on normal environments, can inadvertently incite guarded reactions from natural life, featuring the intricacies of existing together with untamed animals.

Training and mindfulness assume vital parts in limiting the dangers related with creature experiences. Figuring out the ways of behaving, living spaces, and cautioning indications of potential dangers can engage people to go with informed choices and play it safe while exploring conditions where natural life might be available. Protection endeavors pointed toward saving normal living spaces, carrying out dependable the travel industry practices, and cultivating conjunction add to making a harmony between human exercises and the necessities of wild creatures.

5.3: Cultural Perspectives on Clawed Creatures

Social points of view on mauled animals shift generally across various social orders, reflecting assorted convictions, folklores, and representative implications related with these cryptic creatures. From old civilizations to contemporary societies, the depiction of ripped at animals in old stories, religion, craftsmanship, and writing gives knowledge into the human creative mind, fears, and desires. These social viewpoints shape the stories encompassing hooks and add to a rich embroidery of mythic animals, incredible monsters, and representative themes that have persevered through the ages.

In many societies, hooks are significant of force, strength, and basic senses. The picture of an animal with sharp, considerable paws frequently represents untamed powers of nature, the eccentricism of the wild, and the innate risk presented by such animals. These social portrayals draw on the basic apprehension about the obscure and the instinctual acknowledgment of paws as strong instruments of endurance and predation.

In old Egyptian folklore, the goddess Sekhmet is portrayed with the top of a lioness and is much of the time shown bearing long, bended hooks. Sekhmet, related with both annihilation and security, encapsulates the double idea of paws as instruments of both turmoil and request. The lioness, with her sharp hooks, addresses the wild defender of the pharaoh and the vast equilibrium kept up with by the goddess.

The social meaning of paws is additionally obvious in Chinese folklore, where mythical serpents, frequently depicted with tore feet, hold colossal representative significance. Mythical serpents, creatures of incredible influence and intelligence, are loved as images of favorable luck, security, and the grandiose request. The winged serpent's hooks, sharp and powerful, are accepted to have the capacity to avoid underhanded spirits and bring thriving. In this social setting, hooks are not simply weapons yet convey favorable meanings, addressing the altruistic and defensive parts of these legendary animals.

In Hindu folklore, the goddess Durga is one more impressive divinity related with paws. Frequently portrayed riding a tiger or lion, Durga employs different weapons, including sharp paws or nails. The symbolism of Durga's paws is emblematic of her wild defensive nature, as she fights and losses the powers of malevolence. The goddess' numerous arms, each bearing a weapon, including paws, underline her capacity to stand up to and defeat dangers to enormous concordance.

Moving to the old stories of native people groups, the Wendigo of Algonquian customs is a legendary animal related with winter, starvation, and the risks of the wild. Depicted as having stretched appendages and well honed hooks, the Wendigo exemplifies the basic feelings of dread of starvation and the outcomes of surrendering to taboo cravings. In this social setting, the Wendigo's hooks act as images of both actual danger and the ethical perils inborn in the cruel real factors of endurance.

The imagery of hooks isn't bound to fanciful animals; it reaches out to unbelievable creatures and society legends. In Celtic folklore, the legend Cú Chulainn is frequently connected with the legendary animal known as the Cú-Sith, a huge, unearthly canine with fearsome paws. Cú Chulainn himself is famous for his battle ability, and his relationship with an animal highlighting strong paws upgrades his mythic status as a considerable hero.

In Japanese fables, the Tengu is an unbelievable animal frequently portrayed with avian highlights, including long, sharp hooks. Tengu are viewed as the two defenders of the mountains and devilish comedians. The hooks of the Tengu represent their capacity to protect sacrosanct spaces while additionally featuring the fanciful and erratic nature of these heavenly creatures.

The social meaning of hooks reaches out to Local American practices, where the Thunderbird is a strong and magnificent animal related with tempests and lightning.

Portrayed with claws fit for holding thunderclaps, the Thunderbird addresses the crude essential energy tackled by this fanciful being. In this unique situation, the paws of the Thunderbird represent the powers of nature and the extraordinary force of tempests.

In African folklore, the panther is in many cases depicted as a legendary animal with strong paws, exemplifying both beauty and savagery. The panther is respected for its capacity to move quietly and its ability as a tracker. The social imagery of the panther's hooks highlights the characteristics of covertness, strength, and flexibility, filling in as an image of veneration and motivation.

Social points of view on mauled animals likewise manifest in strict convictions and iconography. In Christian imagery, the mythical beast, frequently portrayed with hooks and connected with Satan, addresses the exemplification of malevolence and confusion. The winged serpent's sharp paws represent the damaging powers that Christianity looks to survive. This emblematic theme is apparent in different strict texts, works of art, and building components.

In Norse folklore, the mythical beast Níðhöggr, staying underneath the foundations of Yggdrasil, the World Tree, is portrayed with sharp hooks and a snake like structure. Níðhöggr's paws, alongside its voracious craving, address the disastrous powers undermining the strength of the universe. The imagery of the winged serpent's hooks is woven into the more extensive embroidery of Norse cosmology, where disarray and request are in unending strain.

The social meaning of hooks reaches out to the workmanship and imagery of native people groups all over the planet. In Local American craftsmanship, portrayals of creatures with unmistakable paws, like bears or birds, convey otherworldly importance. These portrayals frequently represent the association among people and the normal world, underscoring the regard and love for the creatures that share a similar climate. The paws of these animals become images of solidarity, security, and the interconnectedness of every single living being.

In contemporary mainstream society, the social viewpoints on ripped at animals keep on advancing. The depiction of werewolves in writing, film, and TV, for instance, draws on the original of people changing into wolf-like creatures with sharp paws during the full moon. This theme, established in old legends and folklores, reflects getting through social apprehensions of the untamed and basic parts of human instinct.

The imagery of hooks additionally tracks down articulation in contemporary tattoo craftsmanship, where plans highlighting pawed animals, like mythical beasts or pumas, are well known decisions. These tattoos frequently pass individual implications related on to strength, flexibility, or an association with mythic stories. The demonstration of embellishing the body with such images mirrors a person's social and individual commitment with the more deeply layers of importance related with hooks.

In East Asian societies, the winged serpent stays a strong image, and portrayals of mythical beasts with sharp hooks keep on holding social importance. Winged serpent moves during Lunar New Year festivities frequently highlight entertainers wearing mythical beast ensembles with intricate paws, underlining the animal's representative job as a harbinger of favorable luck and security against vindictive powers.

In the realm of writing, the social points of view on paws are investigated in works of imagination and sci-fi. Creators frequently attract on mythic themes to make fantastical animals with sharp hooks, adding layers of importance to their accounts. The symbolism of hooks turns into a strong component in narrating, summoning basic impulses, fears, and the persevering through interest with the secrets of the regular world.

Social viewpoints on mauled animals are woven into the texture of human convictions, folklores, and imaginative articulations. Whether representing the defensive powers of divinities, exemplifying the untamed powers of nature, or filling in as themes in contemporary craftsmanship and writing, paws hold an assorted scope of implications across various societies. These points of view enlighten the intricate connection among people and the normal world, catching the creative mind and mirroring the ageless subjects of solidarity, power, and the getting through secrets of nature.

5.4: Documented Claw Injuries and Survival Stories

Reported paw wounds and endurance stories give an arresting look into the crude and frequently dangerous collaborations among people and ripped at animals. From experiences with dominant hunters to startling showdowns with wild creatures, these accounts highlight the flighty idea of the wild and the difficulties people face while exploring imparted conditions to considerable animals furnished with sharp hooks. These accounts enlighten the flexibility of the human soul, the significance of grasping creature conduct, and the perplexing elements intrinsic in existing together with untamed occupants of the normal world.

One of the reported paw wounds that collected global consideration happened in 2003 when a prestigious natural life lover, Timothy Treadwell, and his friend were lethally gone after by a mountain bear in The Frozen North's Katmai Public Park. Treadwell, who burned through broadened periods living among bears and other natural life, meant to encourage understanding and security for these animals. In any case, his closeness to wild bears prompted a grievous experience. The episode underscored the intrinsic dangers related with human-bear associations, particularly when limits between their domains are obscured.

Essentially, the narrative of a lethal tiger assault at the San Francisco Zoo in 2007 stunned the general population. Three young fellows were destroyed by a Siberian tiger after they moved over a wall and entered the tiger nook.

The enormous feline's paws and teeth caused lethal wounds for one of the people, featuring the outcomes of flighty way of behaving and the requirement for tough wellbeing estimates in zoological offices. The occurrence incited reexamination of zoo nooks and guest security conventions.

Endurance stories following hook wounds frequently grandstand the strength and cleverness of people confronting perilous circumstances. Bethany Hamilton's story is a convincing model. In 2003, at 13 years old, Hamilton was gone after by a tiger shark while riding in Hawaii. The shark cut off her left arm, however Hamilton's assurance and love for riding powered her recuperation. Getting back to cutthroat surfing with a hand crafted board, Hamilton turned into a motivation, exhibiting the human ability to beat difficulty and keep seeking after one's interests.

In 2016, a young man fell into the nook of Harambe, a silverback gorilla, at the Cincinnati Zoo. Confronted with the expected danger to the youngster, zoo authorities settled on the hard decision to euthanize Harambe. The occurrence started banters about parental obligation, zoo wellbeing measures, and the moral contemplations of keeping creatures in imprisonment. The experience highlighted the difficulties of dealing with the perplexing elements among people and strong, keen creatures, particularly in hostage settings.

Escapes from imprisonment, while uncommon, have brought about emotional showdowns among people and wild creatures, exhibiting the versatility and senses of animals in unforeseen settings. In 2011, in Zanesville, Ohio, many outlandish creatures, including lions, tigers, and bears, were released by their proprietor before he ended his own life. Policing confronted the overwhelming undertaking of catching or euthanizing the got away from creatures to safeguard public wellbeing. The occurrence focused on the remiss guidelines encompassing the confidential responsibility for creatures and the potential dangers related with their departure.

Reported experiences with venomous animals additionally add to the story of paw wounds. Snakebite episodes, frequently including species with sharp teeth and venomous hooks, feature the dangerous outcomes of human-natural life connections. The endurance stories following snakebites highlight the significance of brief clinical mediation, mindfulness, and preventive estimates in locales where venomous snakes are predominant.

In a striking story of endurance, Australian untamed life master and TV character Steve Irwin confronted a frightening experience with a stingray in 2006. While recording a narrative in the Incomparable Hindrance Reef, Irwin was struck in the chest by a stingray's point, bringing about a deadly injury. The episode shed light on the eccentric idea of associations with marine animals and the inborn dangers looked by the individuals who work intimately with wild creatures.

The account of creature assaults and endurance reaches out to experiences with huge felines, for example, mountain lions or panthers, particularly in areas where human advancement infringes on regular environments.

In 2018, a path sprinter in Colorado endure a mountain lion assault by retaliating with his exposed hands. The man supported wounds to his face, wrist, and arms yet figured out how to kill the mountain lion, delineating the instinctual survival reaction and the perseverance expected to endure such experiences.

In metropolitan conditions, unforeseen experiences with wild creatures feature the versatility of animals to human-adjusted scenes. Reports of bears meandering into rural areas or huge felines lurking city roads highlight the difficulties of off-setting metropolitan advancement with untamed life protection. These occurrences stress the significance of training, mindfulness, and dependable metropolitan wanting to limit clashes among people and wild creatures.

The tale of Inky, an octopus at the Public Aquarium of New Zealand, caught worldwide consideration in 2016 when the shrewd cephalopod figured out how to get away from its walled in area and advance toward opportunity in the Pacific Sea. Inky's getaway exhibited the knowledge and critical abilities to think of octopuses, leaving aquarium staff both dazzled and with a recently discovered regard for the animal's impulses. The getaway brought up issues about the states of imprisonment for profoundly canny and versatile marine creatures.

Endurance stories including experiences with hooks likewise stretch out to the domain of tamed creatures. In 2018, a lady in the US warded off a crazy wildcat that went after her in her carport. The lady, outfitted exclusively with her exposed hands and the senses for self-safeguarding, figured out how to curb the catamount until help showed up. The episode featured the surprising perils that can emerge even in rural settings and the significance of knowing how to answer notwithstanding natural life experiences.

The commonness of archived hook wounds highlights the requirement for public mindfulness, dependable natural life the board, and informed decision-production while exploring conditions imparted to wild animals. Instruction on creature conduct, preventive measures, and appropriate wellbeing conventions add to limiting the dangers related with human-untamed life communications. While endurance stories feature the strength of people confronting hook wounds, the accentuation stays on cultivating conjunction, understanding, and regard for the untamed occupants of the normal world.

In native societies, endurance stories including experiences with wild creatures frequently convey profound social importance. The capacity to explore the indigenous habitat, grasp the ways of behaving of creatures, and answer actually to potential dangers is in many cases gone down through ages. These basic instincts are indispensable to the social personality and flexibility of native networks, featuring the profound association among people and the normal world.

Inuit societies, for instance, have a rich custom of existing together with untamed life in the Cold locales. Endurance accounts of experiences with polar bears, furnished with strong hooks, are woven into the texture of Inuit old stories. The abilities and information expected to explore the Cold scene, expect the developments of polar bears, and guarantee endurance in outrageous circumstances are gone down through oral customs and lived encounters.

Essentially, among native people groups in the Amazon rainforest, endurance stories including experiences with pumas and other pawed animals are fundamental to their social accounts. The complicated comprehension of the backwoods biological system, the ways of behaving of untamed life, and the profound associations with creatures add to the versatility of these networks. The examples gained from endurance stories become piece of the aggregate insight that supports native societies as one with the regular world.

Reported paw wounds and endurance stories offer a diverse viewpoint on the perplexing elements among people and the untamed occupants of nature. From experiences with dominant hunters to surprising showdowns with wild creatures in metropolitan settings, these stories uncover the erratic idea of the wild and the difficulties people face while exploring imparted conditions to animals equipped with sharp paws. While certain accounts bring about misfortune, others exhibit the flexibility of the human soul and the significance of dependable concurrence. These stories highlight the requirement for schooling, mindfulness, and informed decision-production to relieve the dangers related with human-untamed life cooperations and cultivate an amicable relationship with the different occupants of the regular world.

Chapter 6

Human-Claw Interaction

Human-paw collaboration, a powerful transaction among mankind and the considerable weaponry of hooks, embodies a different range of experiences, going from endurance stories to social imagery and logical investigation. This diverse collaboration mirrors the complicated connection among people and the untamed occupants of the normal world, where the extremely sharp extremities of different animals act as the two devices of endurance and subjects of social interest. Analyzing human-paw cooperation divulges accounts of versatility, illustrations gained from the wild, and the getting through effect of hooks on the human mind.

Endurance stories coming from human-hook experiences weave stories of both misfortune and win. In 2003, Timothy Treadwell, an energetic untamed life devotee, and his friend confronted a lethal wild bear assault in The Frozen North's Katmai Public Park. Treadwell's vicinity to wild bears, driven by his central goal to secure and figure out them, brought about an unmistakable representation of the innate risks of close collaborations with dominant hunters. The episode accentuated the critical significance of regarding limits among human and creature domains to forestall lamentable results.

In an alternate setting, the 2016 occurrence at the Cincinnati Zoo including a little fellow falling into the gorilla nook brought the mind boggling elements of human-paw communication to the very front. At the point when a silverback gorilla named Harambe moved toward the youngster, zoo authorities went with the hard decision to euthanize the gorilla to guarantee the kid's wellbeing. The occurrence provoked soul-looking through conversations about the moral ramifications of keeping creatures in bondage, zoo security conventions, and the difficulties of overseeing human-natural life experiences, even in controlled settings.

Endurance stories likewise stretch out to experiences with venomous animals. Snakebites, frequently coming about because of accidental human-hook collaborations, feature the perilous outcomes of such experiences. The endurance stories following snakebites highlight the significance of quick clinical mediation, mindfulness, and preventive estimates in districts where venomous snakes are predominant. The strength of people confronting these unsafe circumstances turns into a demonstration of the human ability to adjust and beat difficulties presented by animals furnished with venomous teeth and paws.

In the marine domain, reported experiences with pawed animals go off in strange directions. In 2006, famous natural life master Steve Irwin confronted a deadly experience with a stingray while shooting a narrative in the Incomparable Hindrance Reef. The spike of the stingray caused a human injury, uncovering the erratic idea of communications with marine animals and the inborn dangers looked by the people who work intimately with wild creatures. Irwin's inheritance underlines the requirement for mindfulness and regard while exploring the territories of animals furnished with extraordinary and possibly risky members.

Escapes from bondage have additionally brought about emotional human-hook cooperations. The 2011 episode in Zanesville, Ohio, where many colorful creatures, including lions and tigers, were released by their proprietor, highlighted the potential dangers related with the confidential responsibility for animals. Policing confronted the difficult assignment of catching or euthanizing the got away from creatures to safeguard public security, featuring the results of human activities on both hostage creatures and the encompassing local area.

The social imagery of hooks rises above endurance accounts, penetrating different parts of human articulation and conviction frameworks. In folklore and legends, paws frequently represent basic senses, power, and the everlasting battle among request and disarray. The goddess Sekhmet in old Egyptian folklore, portrayed with the top of a lioness and sharp paws, typifies both horrendous and defensive powers. The paws of mythical serpents in Chinese folklore represent propitious characteristics, addressing security and favorable luck. These social viewpoints on hooks add to the rich embroidery of human convictions and mythic stories, molding how paws are seen and perceived.

Social imagery encompassing paws is clear in strict iconography also. In Christian imagery, winged serpents frequently portrayed with sharp paws are related with fiendish powers and disorder, underscoring the timeless battle among great and malevolence. Norse folklore highlights winged serpents with hooks too, for example, Níðhöggr, whose sharp paws exemplify disastrous powers compromising infinite strength. The representative utilization of paws in strict settings reflects more profound implications connected with ethical quality, grandiose request, and the powers that shape the human experience.

Social viewpoints on hooks stretch out to craftsmanship and writing, where paws become strong images and story components. In Celtic folklore, the legend Cú Chulainn is related with the Cú-Sith, a ghastly canine with fearsome hooks, upgrading his mythic status as an impressive champion. Japanese old stories includes the Tengu, an animal with avian elements and sharp paws, addressing the two defenders of the mountains and naughty comedians. The symbolism of hooks in imaginative articulations fills in as an extension between social convictions, narrating, and the visual portrayal of mythic animals.

Contemporary mainstream society keeps on drawing motivation according to social points of view on hooks. In the domain of imagination writing and gaming, mythical beasts with sharp hooks typify the prime example of immense, treasure-monitoring snakes. Werewolves, frequently portrayed with sharp hooks, keep on enthralling crowds in writing and film, associating present day accounts to anti-quated legends. The persevering through interest with hooks in mainstream society mirrors the ageless allure of these images and their capacity to summon basic impulses and prototype symbolism.

Logical investigation of hooks dives into the biomechanics, developmental trans-formations, and natural jobs of these imposing designs. Hooks, molded by a long period of time of development, serve different capabilities in the animals of the world collectively, from hunting and safeguard to climbing and route. The investi-gation of paw morphology gives experiences into the natural specialties involved by various species and the manners by which hooks add to their endurance and proliferation.

Remarkable models in nature exhibit the mind blowing variety of hooks and their versatile importance. The retractable hooks of huge felines, like lions and tigers, are fundamental for catching prey and climbing. The strong hooks of bears empower them to scrounge for food and safeguard against expected dangers. The claws of flying predators, similar to falcons and birds of prey, are finely tuned instruments for getting a handle on and getting prey mid-flight. Every species' hooks are finely tuned to its environmental specialty and conduct needs, mirroring the complex dance among structure and capability in the regular world.

Human interest with paws stretches out past the domain of wild animals to the tamed. Felines, for example, have retractable hooks that fill both useful and expressive needs.

These retractable hooks empower them to climb, chase, and guard themselves, while the demonstration of withdrawing and broadening paws is likewise a type of correspondence and self-articulation. The connection among people and trained creatures, like felines, features the convergence of organic variations and the social elements between species.

Hook wounds coming about because of human-creature connections, whether co-incidental or purposeful, highlight the requirement for a nuanced comprehension of creature conduct and legitimate wellbeing precautionary measures. The obligation lies not just with people drawing in with wild or trained creatures yet additionally with establishments that house and show these animals. Zoos, aquariums, and un-tamed life safe-havens assume a significant part in teaching people in general about the regular ways of behaving of creatures and carrying out measures to guarantee the security of the two guests and the creatures in their consideration.

In the field of protection, the investigation of human-hook cooperation stretches out to the conservation of regular natural surroundings and the relief of human-untamed life clashes. As human populaces grow and infringe on wild spaces, clashes unavoidably emerge. Understanding the ways of behaving of creatures equipped with sharp paws is fundamental for carrying out powerful protection techniques that focus on the concurrence of people and natural life. Preservation endeavors point not exclusively to safeguard jeopardized species yet additionally to keep up with the fragile equilibrium of environments and forestall the deficiency of bio-diversity.

The entwining of human and pawed animals in the domains of endurance, culture, craftsmanship, science, and preservation mirrors the intricacy of the connection among mankind and the regular world. The narratives of misfortune and win originating from human-hook experiences act as wake up calls, underlining the significance of regard, mindfulness, and capable conjunction. The representative meaning of hooks in social accounts features their getting through influence on human convictions and articulations, associating antiquated legends to contemporary mainstream society.

Logical investigation extends how we might interpret the biological jobs and developmental transformations of paws, revealing insight into the multifaceted systems that empower various species to flourish in their surroundings. The investigation of paws adds to the more extensive area of science and biology, upgrading our insight into the assorted methodologies utilized by creatures to explore and flourish in nature.

Human-hook connection is a diverse peculiarity that envelops a wide exhibit of encounters and viewpoints. From endurance stories that enlighten the flexibility of the human soul to social imagery that meshes hooks into the texture of fantasy and conviction, the unique exchange among people and ripped at animals is both rich and complex.

As we explore this mind boggling relationship, the illustrations gained from human-hook cooperation become important aides for cultivating capable concurrence, protecting biodiversity, and valuing the untamed magnificence of the regular world.

6.1: Historical Significance of Claws

The verifiable meaning of hooks unfurls as a story woven through the texture of human development, mirroring the complex jobs these considerable extremities have played in molding societies, social orders, and conviction frameworks. From old imagery to down to earth applications in weaponry, the authentic excursion of paws traverses across different human advancements, making a permanent imprint on craftsmanship, religion, fighting, and, surprisingly, the improvement of devices. Investigating the verifiable embroidery of hooks unwinds accounts of force, other-worldliness, and the persevering through interest with these normal weapons.

In antiquated societies, paws held significant emblematic implications, frequently entwined with the otherworldly and legendary domains. The Egyptians, for example, worshipped the goddess Sekhmet, portrayed with the top of a lioness and sharp paws. Sekhmet typified both horrendous and defensive powers, representing the double idea of paws as instruments of disorder and protectors of vast equilibrium. The emblematic utilization of paws in antiquated Egyptian workmanship and strict practices highlights the acknowledgment of these normal weapons as strong images of force and heavenly power.

Essentially, in old Chinese folklore, mythical serpents, frequently portrayed with sharp paws, held massive emblematic importance. Winged serpents were respected as images of supreme power, intelligence, and inestimable request. The mythical serpent's paws, similar to those of the unbelievable animal, represented power, assurance, and the capacity to avoid pernicious powers. The social imagery of mythical beast paws turned out to be profoundly implanted in Chinese workmanship, magnificent formal attire, and compositional components, affecting the visual language of dynastic rule.

The Norse folklore of Scandinavia included winged serpents too, with Níðhöggr being a noticeable model. Níðhöggr, staying underneath the foundations of Yggdrasil, the World Tree, was portrayed with sharp paws and a snake like structure. The imagery of Níðhöggr's paws exemplified the horrendous powers that compromised inestimable steadiness, adding to the rich embroidery of Norse cosmology and mythic accounts. Hooks in Norse folklore filled in as allegories for disarray and the ceaseless battle among request and entropy.

Moving past mythic accounts, authentic societies integrated paws into down to earth parts of day to day existence. Native people groups across the globe used hooks as apparatuses, weapons, and enhancements.

The Inuit, for instance, created apparatuses from the paws of creatures like bears and seals. These executes filled different needs, from slicing and cutting to formal use, mirroring the genius and flexibility of native societies in using normal materials.

In antiquated Rome, the hawk's claws held representative importance as the Roman standard known as the aquila. The aquila, a bird molded image, embellished the Roman legionary guidelines, addressing the tactical ability and distinction of the army. The hawk's claws holding a thunderclap represented the quick and strong nature of Roman military may. The utilization of hooks in this setting represents how normal components were integrated into the imagery of military emblem to move dedication and convey strength.

In middle age Europe, the heraldic custom highlighted different animals with hooks as images on emblems. Lions, griffins, and other legendary animals with sharp paws decorated safeguards, flags, and defensive layer, meaning the honorable temperances of mental fortitude, strength, and bravery. The joining of hooks into heraldry stressed the association between the normal world and the goals of valor, making a visual language that imparted both heredity and military ability.

The verifiable meaning of paws reaches out to the domain of weaponry, where the consolidation of sharp limbs into edges and defensive layer turned into an essential decision in different societies. The kukri, a particular blade with a forward-bending sharp edge and sharp, internal confronting edge, has been generally connected with the Gurkha fighters of Nepal. The kukri's plan, with an articulated tip looking like a paw, fills both down to earth and emblematic needs. It is a flexible device for every-day undertakings, a weapon in battle, and a social image addressing the grit and strength of the Gurkha champions.

With regards to antiquated Rome, the combatants used weapons with sharp places and edges, frequently looking like the paws of wild creatures. The plan of gladiatorial weapons, including the spear and the retiarius' net and pike mix, re-flected the base idea of battle and the relationship of warriors with the untamed powers of nature. The utilization of such weapons in the field highlighted the showiness and imagery of gladiatorial battle, with paws filling in as the two devices of annihilation and components of scene.

The authentic meaning of hooks in weaponry additionally arises in East Asian military customs. Customary hand to hand fighting in China, Japan, and other Asian societies frequently consolidate paw like methods, enlivened by the develop-ments of creatures with sharp hooks. Styles like Baguazhang, enlivened by the round developments of the mythical serpent, and Falcon Paw Kung Fu, imitating the hold-ing movements of a bird's claws, feature the impact of regular structures on hand to hand fighting procedures. The fuse of hook motivated developments improves both the functional adequacy and the emblematic profundity of these military customs.

In native societies, verifiable importance arises in the customs and functions where hooks assume a part in profound practices. Command hierarchies among Local American clans highlight creatures with sharp paws, addressing family affilia-tions, gatekeeper spirits, and hereditary associations. The cut portrayals of hooks on command hierarchies act as visual illustrations for the qualities, ethics, and stories related with every family, adding to the conservation of social character and legacy.

The authentic meaning of paws in antiquated medication and speculative chem-istry mirrors the convergence of regular imagery and pragmatic applications. In archaic Europe, the faith in the teaching of marks set that the actual qualities of plants and creatures were demonstrative of their restorative properties. Hooks, with their sharp and considerable appearance, were remembered to have remedial abilities. Substances got from paws, like powdered hooks or concentrates, were inte-grated into restorative creations with the conviction that they could treat sicknesses related with strength, essentialness, or dexterity.

By and large, paws have been utilized in the production of stylized and cere-monial items, underscoring their emblematic and otherworldly importance. In Local American societies, stately veils cut from wood frequently highlight portrayals of creatures with unmistakable hooks, addressing profound creatures and familial associations. The utilization of hooks in such creative articulations highlights their job in conveying social stories, otherworldly convictions, and a profound veneration for the regular world.

The authentic meaning of paws likewise meets with the specialty of decoration. Hooks, especially those of creatures considered sacrosanct or strong, have been designed into gems, special necklaces, and charms across societies. In old Egypt, gems embellished with portrayals of lion paws mirrored the representative relationship with Sekhmet and the defensive characteristics credited to the goddess. In native societies, paw gems filled in as images of status, profound association, and individual strengthening.

The imagery of hooks stretches out to strict iconography, where the symbolism of heavenly creatures and legendary animals frequently integrates sharp extremities. Hindu divinities, like Goddess Durga, are portrayed with paws or sharp weapons in their different arms, representing their ability to battle malicious powers and keep grandiose control. The relationship of paws with divine creatures mirrors the acknowledgment of these regular weapons as images of solidarity, insurance, and the capacity to defeat misfortune.

In middle age Christian craftsmanship, mythical beasts frequently portrayed with sharp paws represent the powers of fiendishness and turmoil that Christianity tries to survive. The mythical serpent, with its sharp paws and fearsome appearance, turned into a visual portrayal of the wicked enemies that holy people and upright figures won over. The representative utilization of hooks in strict craftsmanship mirrors the more extensive social view of these limbs as images of danger and resistance.

The authentic meaning of hooks with regards to hunting and endurance apparatuses is obvious in ancient curios and archeological revelations. Early human networks used hooks as parts of apparatuses, whether appended to wooden handles or designed into executes for cutting, cutting, or hunting. The versatility of hooks as apparatuses, especially without any metalworking advancements, highlights their useful importance in day to day existence.

Paws as devices likewise tracked down articulation in native hunting customs. The usage of creature paws in making weapons, like bolts or lances, added to the adequacy of hunting systems. The joining of hooks into hunting devices mirrors the genius and resourcefulness of native networks in using regular materials to meet their reasonable requirements.

In the domain of writing, authentic importance is obvious in the accounts that component hooks as emblematic components or topical themes. The amazing stories of legends doing combating winged serpents, animals with sharp paws, have pervaded social accounts across civic establishments. Whether as Beowulf going up against the winged serpent or Holy person George killing the mythical beast, these accounts mirror the immortal human interest with the showdown between mortal creatures and strong, mauled foes.

In Chinese writing, winged serpents with sharp paws are repetitive figures in mythic stories and fables. These winged serpents, frequently portrayed as kind-hearted defenders or shrewd creatures, typify social goals and convey moral examples. The depiction of winged serpents with sharp paws in writing turns into a figurative investigation of force, shrewdness, and the sensitive harmony among generosity and malice.

The verifiable meaning of paws is likewise manifest in the investigation of the regular world. Early naturalists and pilgrims recorded the paws of fascinating animals experienced during their excursions, adding to the growing collection of information about the variety of life on The planet. The point by point perceptions of hooks, alongside other physical highlights, laid the foundation for the logical comprehension of species and their transformations.

With regards to fossil science, the investigation of paws has given experiences into the transformative history of different species. Fossilized stays of old animals, including dinosaurs and ancient warm blooded creatures, frequently incorporate all around saved paws. The examination of these fossils adds to how we might interpret the natural jobs, ways of behaving, and variations of antiquated life forms. Paws, as saved in the fossil record, act as windows into the developmental past and the complex transaction among structure and capability.

The verifiable meaning of paws takes on a worldwide viewpoint as the investigation of normal assets and shipping lanes carried experiences with colorful animals. The hooks of creatures from far off lands became sought-after items, esteemed for their unique case and saw remedial properties.

The exchange hooks, whether from huge felines, bears, or marine animals, turned out to be important for a bigger monetary and social trade, impacting the improvement of exchange organizations and adding to the social trade between civic establishments.

The verifiable meaning of paws is a rich embroidery woven through the chronicles of human development. From old imagery to commonsense applications in weaponry, hooks play played different parts across societies and time spans. Whether filling in as images of force in fanciful stories, down to earth apparatuses in day to day existence, or parts of weaponry in military customs, hooks have made a permanent imprint on the human experience. The interest with hooks, established in both useful need and representative profundity, keeps on reverberating in contemporary culture, associating current points of view with the getting through tradition of these impressive members.

6.2: Symbolism in Art and Literature

Imagery in workmanship and writing, a significant and widespread language, rises above social limits and ages, winding around complicated stories that reverberate with the profundities of the human mind. Whether communicated through visual show-stoppers or the composed word, imagery mixes significance into the conventional, changing the unremarkable into the exceptional. Investigating the rich embroidery of imagery uncovers how specialists and journalists saddle the influence of similitude, moral story, and visual themes to convey significant bits of insight, incite contemplation, and summon a heap of feelings.

In visual expressions, imagery tracks down articulation through the purposeful utilization of pictures, varieties, and structures to convey dynamic ideas, feelings, or cultural discourse. From the beginning of time, specialists have utilized images to impart complex thoughts that frequently rise above the constraints of language. One of the most notable instances of imagery in workmanship is the utilization of strict imagery during the Renaissance, where painters like Leonardo da Vinci and Michelangelo utilized figurative themes to convey profound subjects.

Leonardo da Vinci's "The Last Dinner" fills in as a show-stopper of strict imagery. The creation catches the second when Jesus declares the selling out by one of his pupils during the last feast. The emblematic utilization of signals, articulations, and position of figures conveys more profound implications — from the dismal hand token of Judas to the tranquil face of Christ. The position of figures in a three-sided piece, an image of the Heavenly Trinity, adds a layer of religious importance. Through careful imagery, da Vinci changes a scriptural story into a visual reflection on trust, treachery, and reclamation.

Also, Michelangelo's frescoes in the Sistine House of prayer are loaded with emblematic symbolism. The famous picture of God contacting contact Adam's finger in "The Formation of Adam" exemplifies significant religious imagery, representing the heavenly flash of life granted to humankind.

The utilization of lively varieties, physical accuracy, and spatial creation upgrades the profound effect and religious reverberation of the fine art. The mind boggling exchange of imagery in these magnum opuses hoists the visual experience past simple portrayal, welcoming watchers into a scrutinizing commitment with significant thoughts.

Moving past strict settings, imagery in workmanship stretches out to cultural critique and political articulation. The utilization of purposeful anecdote and allegory permits craftsmen to investigate or ridicule winning accepted practices, power designs, and shameful acts. Francisco Goya's "The Third of May 1808" is a strong illustration of political imagery. Portraying the execution of Spanish regular citizens by French fighters during the Peninsular Conflict, the artistic creation catches the severity of war and the obstruction of the person against abusive powers. The glaring difference between the enlightened figure in white and the unremarkable terminating crew represents the strain among honesty and state-endorsed brutality, making a strong enemy of war proclamation.

In the late nineteenth and mid twentieth hundreds of years, the Symbolist development arose as a response against the realism and authenticity of the time. Symbolist specialists, like Gustav Klimt and Odilon Redon, tried to summon feelings and pass profound insights on through emblematic and illusory symbolism. Klimt's "The Kiss" is a quintessential illustration of Symbolist craftsmanship, where gold leaf, mathematical examples, and interweaved figures represent subjects of affection, otherworldliness, and the extraordinary idea of human association.

In the domain of writing, imagery unfurls as a story device that goes past the strict and investigates the profundities of human experience. Scholars use images to permeate their works with layers of significance, welcoming perusers to participate in a nuanced translation of the text. F. Scott Fitzgerald's "The Incomparable Gatsby" is an exemplary illustration of scholarly imagery. Approval toward the finish of Daisy Buchanan's dock fills in as a powerful image, addressing Gatsby's out of reach dream and the tricky idea of the Pursuit of happiness itself. The imagery typifies subjects of goal, bafflement, and the perplexing interaction among deception and reality.

The utilization of imagery in writing isn't restricted to direct moral stories; rather, it works on a range that envelops both express and more nuanced structures. In George Orwell's "Animal Homestead," the actual ranch turns into a representative microcosm of the Soviet Association subject to Stalin's authority. The animals address various classes and political figures, while the homestead's change reflects the cultural movements that happened during the Russian Upset. Orwell's utilization of animal characters and homestead settings fills in as a moral story that studies despotism, power elements, and the control of philosophy.

In the class of mystical authenticity, imagery takes on a dreamlike quality, obscuring the limits between the fantastical and the commonplace.

Gabriel García Márquez's "100 Years of Isolation" is a fundamental work that entwines otherworldly components with a profoundly emblematic story. The common theme of yellow butterflies, for example, represents the recurrent idea of time and the interconnected fates of the Buendía family. Márquez's utilization of imagery advances the account with layers of significance, welcoming perusers to investigate the perplexing embroidered artwork of memory, history, and the human condition.

Contemporary writing keeps on utilizing imagery as a strong narrating gadget. In J.K. Rowling's "Harry Potter" series, the repetitive theme of the phoenix fills in as an image of resurrection, versatility, and the recurrent idea of life. The phoenix's capacity to ascend from its remains reflects the characters' excursions of conquering affliction and tracking down trust notwithstanding haziness. Rowling's capable utilization of imagery adds profundity to the fantastical universe of wizards and enchanted animals, reverberating with perusers on a general and close to home level.

Imagery in writing likewise stretches out to social and philosophical investigations. Haruki Murakami's book "Kafka on the Shore" digs into the domain of dreams, transcendentalism, and the interconnectedness of the real world and creative mind. The utilization of images, for example, the perplexing fish and the idea of "kafkaesque," adds layers of significance to the story. Murakami's mixing of the dreamlike and the conventional welcomes perusers into a pensive space where images become channels for investigating the secrets of presence.

Past the domain of high writing, imagery pervades mainstream society, including film and TV. Christopher Nolan's film "Commencement" works on numerous layers of imagery, involving the idea of dreams inside dreams as an illustration for the psyche and the obscured limits among the real world and deception. The turning top toward the finish of the film turns into a strong image, welcoming watchers to scrutinize the idea of discernment and the emotional experience of the real world.

The universe of music is another domain where imagery assumes a huge part. In Bounce Dylan's melody "Blowin' in the Breeze," the common inquiry "How frequently should a man turn upward before he can see the sky?" fills in as a representative investigation into the journey for equity, opportunity, and social change. Dylan's verses, described by their wonderful reverberation, draw in with widespread subjects using representative language, welcoming audience members to consider the human condition.

Strict and legendary imagery, well established in social accounts, likewise pervades imaginative articulations. Crafted by William Blake, an eighteenth century writer and craftsman, are saturated with Christian imagery.

Blake's enlightened prints, for example, those from "The Marriage of Paradise and Damnation," include legendary and metaphorical figures that represent profound arousing, the battle among alternate extremes, and the mission for greatness. Blake's utilization of representative language and symbolism turned into a forerunner to the Heartfelt development, impacting ensuing ages of specialists and essayists.

In Eastern practices, strict imagery tracks down articulation in old style writing and workmanship. The Chinese work of art "Excursion toward the West," credited to Wu Cheng'en, is a rich embroidery of imagery that mixes Buddhist lessons, people legends, and figurative stories. The Monkey Lord, Sun Wukong, fills in as a representative figure addressing the excursion of self-revelation and edification. The roundabout design of the story, loaded up with fantastical experiences and moral examples, mirrors the emblematic idea of the journey for profound arousing.

The exchange of imagery in workmanship and writing rises above geological and worldly limits, associating unique societies and ages through shared human encounters. In African writing, Chinua Achebe's "Things Go to pieces" uses representative themes to investigate the impact of customary Igbo culture with pioneer powers. The representative load of the hero Okonkwo's terrible destiny turns into an impression of the more extensive social disturbances and the conflict between native conviction frameworks and outside impacts.

Imagery in workmanship and writing additionally meets with the investigation of personality, especially with regards to postcolonial stories. Salman Rushdie's "12 PM's Youngsters" winds around an embroidery of representative themes that typify the wild history of post-freedom India. The hero Saleem Sinai's otherworldly capacities and the more extensive subject of "12 PM's Kids" represent the exceptional personality and fate of an age brought into the world right now of India's freedom.

The utilization of imagery stretches out to orientation, where craftsmen and journalists utilize emblematic symbolism to investigate and challenge cultural standards. In Virginia Woolf's "Orlando," the hero's orientation change fills in as a representative investigation of character, time, and the ease of selfhood. Woolf's story energetically draws in with the emblematic potential outcomes of orientation, welcoming perusers to think about the developed idea of personality and the manners by which it is formed by social assumptions.

The LGBTQ+ development has likewise embraced imagery for the purpose of portrayal and support. The rainbow banner, embraced as an image of LGBTQ+ pride, integrates a range of varieties to commend variety and consideration. The banner's imagery reaches out past its visual portrayal, filling in as a strong token that resounds with people looking for perceivability, acknowledgment, and confirmation of their personalities.

6.3: Conservation and Protection Efforts

Preservation and security endeavors address a worldwide reaction to the heightening dangers confronting biodiversity and environments. Despite environment annihilation, environmental change, contamination, and the overexploitation of regular assets, people, networks, state run administrations, and associations are meeting up to shield the planet's rich woven artwork of life. The assorted systems and drives utilized in protection endeavors highlight the dire need to offset human exercises with the safeguarding of biological respectability, advancing economical concurrence with the normal world.

Safeguarded regions, incorporating public parks, natural life stores, and marine safe-havens, stand as strongholds of biodiversity conservation. These assigned zones act as shelters for vegetation, offering safe environments where species can flourish without the prompt dangers presented by human exercises. The foundation and upkeep of safeguarded regions are fundamental parts of preservation endeavors, giving shelters to imperiled species, protecting critical biological systems, and cultivating the general wellbeing of the planet.

One notable illustration of effective preservation through safeguarded regions is the Yellowstone Public Park in the US. Laid out in 1872, Yellowstone holds the differentiation of being the primary public park around the world. Its creation denoted a critical crossroads throughout the entire existence of preservation, starting a trend for the foundation of safeguarded regions around the world. Yellowstone's different environments support a wide exhibit of animal categories, including wolves, wild bears, and crowds of buffalo. The recreation area's preservation achievement exhibits the versatility of environments when managed the cost of assurance, displaying the positive effect of safeguarding regular spaces for people in the future.

Marine safeguarded regions assume a urgent part in defending the world's seas and the bunch life structures they support. The Incomparable Boundary Reef Marine Park in Australia remains as a demonstration of deliberate protection endeavors in marine conditions. The Incomparable Obstruction Reef, an UNESCO World Legacy site, is the world's biggest coral reef framework, lodging an unrivaled variety of marine species. The foundation of the marine park, combined with continuous protection drives, tries to relieve the effects of environmental change, coral blanching, and overfishing, guaranteeing the drawn out reasonability of this phenomenal biological system.

Local area based preservation drives perceive the essential job of neighborhood networks in the security of regular assets. Engaging people group to effectively take part in preservation endeavors cultivates a feeling of stewardship, adjusting protection objectives to the necessities and goals of the individuals who occupy the scenes. In Namibia, the collective conservancy model has arisen as a fruitful way to deal with natural life protection.

By conceding neighborhood networks the privileges to oversee and profit from natural life assets, this model boosts the preservation of notable species like elephants and lions. The financial advantages got from capable the travel industry and maintainable normal asset the board add to the general prosperity of networks while cultivating an agreeable concurrence among individuals and natural life.

Preservation endeavors are progressively educated by logical exploration and mechanical advancements. The utilization of state of the art instruments, like satellite checking, remote detecting, and DNA investigation, upgrades how we might interpret biological systems and species elements. These advancements help in following untamed life developments, evaluating natural surroundings changes, and recognizing arising dangers. In the domain of hereditary qualities, propels in DNA examination empower specialists to concentrate on populace elements, hereditary variety, and relatedness among people, giving basic bits of knowledge to viable preservation methodologies.

In the domain of hereditary qualities, propels in DNA examination empower analysts to concentrate on populace elements, hereditary variety, and relatedness among people, giving basic experiences to powerful protection techniques.

Passage protection addresses an essential way to deal with moderating the effects of living space discontinuity. As human advancement pieces regular scenes, making confined patches of living space, natural life passages offer imperative associations between these divided regions. These hallways empower the development of species, working with quality stream, movement, and admittance to assets. The Banff Public Park in Canada embodies fruitful hall preservation, where untamed life bridges and underpasses permit creatures like wild bears, wolves, and elk to securely navigate the Trans-Canada Expressway. The execution of natural life hallways encourages biological network, fundamental for the drawn out endurance of different species.

Worldwide cooperation is fundamental in tending to preservation challenges that rise above borders. Peaceful accords and shows give systems to helpful endeavors to safeguard biodiversity on a planetary scale. The Show on Organic Variety (CBD), laid out in 1992, addresses a milestone global settlement pointed toward saving natural variety, advancing supportable utilization of normal assets, and guaranteeing the fair and evenhanded sharing of advantages got from hereditary assets. The CBD highlights the interconnectedness of worldwide environments and the common obligation of countries in saving the world's biodiversity.

In the domain of marine preservation, the Antarctic Settlement Framework embodies global collaboration in protecting a special and delicate environment. The Antarctic district, represented by the Antarctic Settlement and its connected arrangements, assigns the region as a logical safeguard, disallows military exercises, and lays out guidelines to forestall ecological debasement.

The cooperative endeavors of countries participated in Antarctic examination highlight the obligation to protecting this unblemished wild, recognizing its worldwide importance.

Preservation drives reach out past earthly and marine environments to address the dire difficulties looked by freshwater living spaces. Streams, lakes, and wetlands are basic parts of the worldwide water cycle and harbor interesting biodiversity. The Ramsar Show, laid out in 1971, centers around the preservation and manageable utilization of wetlands around the world. Ramsar destinations, assigned under the show, address areas of global significance for the preservation of wetland biodiversity. The acknowledgment of wetlands as imperative biological systems highlights the need to safeguard these regions from contamination, territory misfortune, and over-extraction of water assets.

Tending to the effects of environmental change is a vital part of contemporary protection endeavors. Environmental change presents extraordinary difficulties to biological systems, prompting shifts in species disseminations, adjusted phenology, and expanded recurrence of outrageous climate occasions. Protection methodologies currently integrate environment transformation and alleviation measures to improve the strength of biological systems and species. The idea of environment brilliant protection accentuates proactive methodologies that think about the unique idea of biological systems despite environment fluctuation.

Reforestation and afforestation drives assume an essential part in environment savvy protection by sequestering carbon, reestablishing debased scenes, and giving territory to biodiversity. The Bonn Challenge, sent off in 2011, means to reestablish 350 million hectares of corrupted and deforested land by 2030. This worldwide exertion assembles nations, associations, and networks to add to the rebuilding of timberland environments, moderating the effects of deforestation and land corruption.

Imaginative preservation finance systems offer new roads for supporting biodiversity protection. Installments for biological system administrations (PES) address a methodology where people or elements pay for the advantages got from environments, like clean water, carbon sequestration, or natural surroundings conservation. PES drives boost landowners and networks to take part in preservation rehearses that add to the supportable administration of normal assets. The reception of market-based systems, for example, biodiversity balances and green securities, further expands subsidizing hotspots for protection projects, advancing monetary manageability in the field of biodiversity preservation.

Preservation endeavors likewise stretch out to the domain of jeopardized species security and recuperation. The Worldwide Association for Protection of Nature (IUCN) Red Rundown fills in as a thorough asset that evaluates the worldwide termination risk status of thousands of species. The ID of imperiled and fundamentally jeopardized species illuminates designated protection activities, going from environment rebuilding to hostage reproducing programs.

The protection example of overcoming adversity of the California condor epitomizes the effect of devoted recuperation endeavors. When near the precarious edge of elimination, concentrated hostage rearing and renewed introduction programs have prompted a slow expansion in condor populaces, displaying the potential for species recuperation through cooperative preservation measures.

Public mindfulness and training are necessary parts of effective preservation drives. Drawing in networks and cultivating a feeling of obligation for ecological stewardship add to the drawn out progress of preservation endeavors. Instructive projects, nature stores, and ecotourism drives assume critical parts in associating individuals with the regular world, cultivating a more profound appreciation for biodiversity and environments.

Preservation schooling reaches out to bringing issues to light about the unlawful natural life exchange, an unavoidable danger to numerous species. Poaching and dealing of natural life items, driven by interest for outlandish pets, customary drugs, and extravagance products, present extreme dangers to various species, including elephants, rhinoceroses, and pangolins. Worldwide coordinated efforts, for example, the Show on Global Exchange Imperiled Types of Wild Fauna and Verdure (Refers to), look to control and battle unlawful untamed life exchange, guaranteeing the insurance of jeopardized species from double-dealing.

The job of native information and conventional environmental practices in protection couldn't possibly be more significant. Native people group frequently have significant bits of knowledge into maintainable asset the board, biodiversity protection, and versatility to natural changes. Perceiving and regarding native privileges and information frameworks are central to comprehensive and successful protection systems. Native drove preservation drives, for example, the Native Watchmen programs in Canada, engage nearby networks to assume dynamic parts in safeguarding their genealogical grounds and saving conventional natural information.

Innovation, when tackled for protection, opens new outskirts for checking, examination, and public commitment. Camera traps, satellite symbolism, and acoustic checking gadgets give important information to concentrating on untamed life conduct, populace elements, and environment wellbeing. Resident science drives influence the force of public cooperation, permitting people to contribute perceptions, gather information, and participate in preservation endeavors. Stages like iNaturalist and eBird empower individuals overall to become resident researchers, adding to an aggregate comprehension of biodiversity dissemination and overflow.

The combination of protection endeavors with reasonable improvement objectives (SDGs) mirrors an all encompassing way to deal with tending to ecological difficulties while advancing human prosperity. The Unified Countries' 2030 Plan for Reasonable Improvement incorporates explicit objectives connected with biodiversity preservation, environment activity, clean water, and dependable utilization.

Perceiving the interconnectedness of natural and social issues, the SDGs stress the significance of offsetting protection targets with destitution mitigation, orientation correspondence, and social value.

6.4: Human Efforts to Mimic Claw Functions

Human endeavors to impersonate hook capabilities address a captivating crossing point of mechanical development, bio-propelled plan, and the journey for upgrading human capacities. Drawing motivation from the proficiency and flexibility of hooks saw in different creature species, architects and specialists have left on attempts to repeat and coordinate these normal plans into counterfeit frameworks. The investigation of hook propelled innovations traverses assorted fields, from mechanical technology and clinical gadgets to modern applications, mirroring the potential for bridling nature's inventiveness to address human difficulties.

In the domain of mechanical technology, bio-enlivened paws have turned into a point of convergence for creating capable and versatile automated hands. The multifaceted designs and functionalities of regular hooks, developed more than large number of years, act as plans for making mechanical members equipped for controlling items with accuracy and adaptability. The lobster's hook, famous for its solidarity and productivity, has motivated the plan of delicate mechanical grippers that impersonate the adaptability and flexibility of their organic partners. These grippers, frequently produced using elastomeric materials, can adjust to the state of articles, considering secure and delicate getting a handle on, especially in sensitive undertakings or conditions where unbending mechanical technology might be unrealistic.

Specialists have additionally investigated the utilization of biomimetic paws in the advancement of prosthetic appendages and exoskeletons. By copying the biomechanics of regular paws, engineers expect to upgrade the usefulness and normal development of fake appendages, working on the personal satisfaction for people with appendage misfortune. Prosthetic hands consolidating paw enlivened systems give clients a more noteworthy scope of movement and the capacity to perform complicated errands, like getting a handle on little items or composing on a console. The coordination of these biomimetic plans upgrades the pragmatic parts of prosthetics as well as adds to the mental prosperity and feeling of epitome for clients.

In the field of clinical gadgets, paw motivated advancements are gaining ground in negligibly obtrusive medical procedure and designated mediations. The mantis shrimp, known for its strong and quick clipping extremities, has impacted the plan of automated careful devices equipped for exact and proficient developments. These apparatuses, furnished with hook like elements, empower specialists to carry out perplexing systems with upgraded aptitude and decreased obtrusiveness. The utilization of bio-roused hooks in clinical advanced mechanics lines up fully intent on working on careful results, limiting patient injury, and growing the opportunities for complex mediations.

Paw propelled plans reach out into the domain of modern applications, where the requirement for productive and versatile grasping systems is fundamental. The Kingfisher bird, with its quick and exact jumping movement to get prey, has enlivened the improvement of a bio-roused mechanical gripper for modern pick-and-spot errands. Mirroring the Kingfisher's nose, the mechanical gripper uses a smoothed out shape and a shrewd control framework to accomplish quick and exact item control. This use of biomimicry in modern mechanization grandstands the potential for improving productivity and decreasing energy utilization in assembling processes.

The investigation of paw capabilities in materials science has prompted the improvement of imaginative materials and coatings with upgraded holding capacities. The minute designs tracked down on the feet of geckos, known as setae, have propelled the formation of gecko-motivated cements. These cements, described by their capacity to stick to different surfaces and segregate easily, track down applications in advanced mechanics, climbing gadgets, and modern grip. The biomimetic plan of these materials, drawing motivation from the effective grasping systems saw in nature, offers answers for difficulties connected with bond and grinding in different settings.

Nature's paw plans have additionally affected the advancement of state of the art innovations for investigation and salvage missions. The spear like limbs of the bolt worm, a marine invertebrate, have roused the plan of mechanical getting a handle on components for catching items in testing submerged conditions. The flexibility and accuracy of these bio-roused getting a handle on devices hold guarantee for applications in remote ocean investigation, submerged paleontology, and search-and-salvage missions.

In the domain of biomimetic designing, analysts are investigating the reconciliation of savvy materials and computerized reasoning to make versatile paw like designs. The capacity of specific creatures to regulate the solidness and state of their hooks because of various undertakings has enlivened the improvement of fake paws with shape-moving abilities. These brilliant hooks, outfitted with sensors and actuators, can progressively change their morphology to enhance grasp and control in view of the properties of the articles being taken care of. The fuse of man-made brainpower calculations further upgrades the versatility and learning capacities of these biomimetic frameworks.

The investigation of hook capabilities in nature has additionally motivated headways in the field of delicate mechanical technology, where malleable and adaptable materials imitate the attributes of organic tissues. Delicate automated paws, demonstrated after the flexible yet solid designs saw in different creatures, offer benefits in applications where conventional unbending advanced mechanics might restrict. These delicate hooks can adjust to complex shapes, explore restricted spaces, and collaborate securely with fragile items. The adaptability of delicate advanced mechanics, motivated by the biomechanics of regular paws, holds guarantee for applications in clinical gadgets, wearable innovation, and human-robot communication.

Analysts are progressively investigating the capability of 3D printing innovations to imitate complex hook structures with accuracy. The flexibility of 3D printing considers the diversion of many-sided calculations tracked down in normal paws, empowering the creation of tweaked and proficient automated parts. This added substance fabricating approach works with the quick prototyping of bio-enlivened plans, speeding up the turn of events and execution of paw imitating innovations across different enterprises.

The use of biomimetic paws in advanced mechanics and designing isn't restricted to earthbound conditions; it reaches out to aeronautical and space investigation. The claws of raptors, like birds and falcons, have motivated the plan of automated grippers for flying robots. These grippers, furnished with claw like elements, empower robots to handle and move objects with accuracy, impersonating the hunting ability of their avian partners. With regards to space investigation, the investigation of hook capabilities in microorganisms and extremophiles advises the plan regarding automated gadgets for extraterrestrial missions, where versatility to cruel circumstances is fundamental.

While human endeavors to imitate paw capabilities have yielded noteworthy innovative headways, the moral contemplations encompassing bio-roused plans warrant cautious examination. The mindful mix of biomimetic advances includes contemplations of ecological effect, creature government assistance, and the expected results of duplicating nature's plans for human purposes. Finding some kind of harmony among development and moral stewardship is fundamental to guarantee that biomimetic innovations contribute emphatically to human advancement while regarding the standards of manageability and biological honesty.

The investigation of paw capabilities in the normal world has ignited a rush of development across different fields, from mechanical technology and clinical gadgets to modern applications and materials science. The mimicry of hook plans, informed by the proficiency and flexibility saw in different creature species, has prompted forward leaps in innovation that improve human abilities and address complex difficulties. As scientists keep on disentangling the complexities of hook capabilities in nature, the potential for bio-enlivened plans to shape the fate of designing and mechanical technology stays a demonstration of the significant examples that can be gathered from the normal world. The combination of science and innovation opens new wildernesses for investigation, revelation, and the supportable conjunction of human advancement with the perplexing plans idealized by development north of millions of years.

Proceeding with the investigation of biomimetic paws and their applications in human innovation, it's fundamental to dig into explicit models that grandstand the different and effective manners by which analysts and specialists draw motivation from nature's ripped at ponders.

One convincing area of biomimicry is the improvement of dexterous and versatile automated frameworks demonstrated after the biomechanics of creatures with momentous paw capabilities. The mantis shrimp, known for its remarkable ability to strike and complex limbs, has roused the production of bio-enlivened automated arms.

Specialists mean to duplicate the mantis shrimp's ability to hit with amazing velocity and power, imagining applications in fields like submerged investigation, where accuracy and power are significant.

The development of delicate mechanical technology addresses a change in perspective in designing, drawing motivation from the flexibility and flexibility of normal hooks. Delicate mechanical grippers, roused by the mastery of an octopus' limbs or a snake's choking loops, offer another boondocks in human-robot communication. These grippers, frequently produced using adaptable materials, can gently control objects of fluctuating shapes and sizes, making them ideal for applications in conditions where customary unbending robots might be illogical or represent a gamble.

In the clinical field, the mission to upgrade surgeries and clinical mediations has prompted the improvement of bio-motivated apparatuses with hook like functionalities. The Kingfisher bird, with its quick and exact jumping movement to get prey, has affected the plan of clinical instruments for insignificantly obtrusive medical procedures. Getting from the Kingfisher's bill, these instruments are designed for accuracy and productivity, lessening injury to the patient and working on the general progress of medical procedures.

The investigation of biomimetic paws reaches out to the minute domain, where analysts hope to recreate the cement properties of gecko feet for inventive applications. Gecko-roused glues, intended to impersonate the setae on gecko toes, have tracked down their direction into different businesses. From climbing robots that can scale walls and roofs to glue tapes that give reusable and buildup free staying, the potential outcomes are huge. The capacity to make powerful cements without depending on conventional pastes or tapes features the potential for manageable and harmless to the ecosystem arrangements.

Progressions in material science have been crucial in reproducing the primary properties of paws. The use of composite materials, propelled by the flexibility and strength of normal paws, has suggestions for the aviation and auto ventures. The joining of lightweight yet hearty materials in the development of airplane parts or vehicle parts adds to eco-friendliness, decreased natural effect, and improved underlying uprightness.

The investigation of biomimetic paws isn't bound to Earth; it reaches out to the domain of room investigation. The plan of mechanical arms for space meanderers, propelled by the flexibility and holding skill of hooks in different earthly creatures, assumes a critical part in extraterrestrial missions. These mechanical arms, furnished with paw like highlights, empower the exact control of devices, test assortment, and different assignments fundamental for logical investigation on heavenly bodies.

In the field of exoskeletons and wearable innovation, analysts are drawing motivation from the biomechanics of normal hooks to improve human capacities. Exoskeletons furnished with biomimetic getting a handle on systems can give people expanded strength and skill, possibly supporting exercises that require both accuracy and power. This application holds guarantee for helping people with portability challenges, as well as enlarging the actual capacities of laborers in enterprises that request hard work or unpredictable undertakings.

The mix of computerized reasoning (man-made intelligence) and AI into biomimetic paws addresses an outskirts of development. Scientists are investigating how simulated intelligence calculations can improve the flexibility and learning capacities of automated hooks. By empowering these frameworks to progressively change their hold and control techniques in view of constant information and criticism, the potential for independent and canny mechanical frameworks becomes evident. This union of biomimicry and artificial intelligence opens roads for making machines that can learn and develop their capacities after some time.

Moral contemplations assume a pivotal part in the turn of events and organization of biomimetic paw innovations. As people endeavor to emulate the productivity and flexibility of normal paws, questions emerge about the moral ramifications of utilizing bio-motivated plans for different purposes. Guaranteeing that these innovations stick to standards of manageability, ecological obligation, and regard for biodiversity is fundamental. Finding some kind of harmony between mechanical advancement and moral stewardship is foremost to tackling the capability of biomimetic hooks while limiting potentially negative results.

The cooperative idea of biomimicry, where specialists, designers, and scientists cooperate, mirrors an all encompassing way to deal with development. Biomimetic plans are not simple impersonations yet rather incorporations of normal standards into human-made frameworks. This cooperative collaboration between disciplines accentuates the significance of interdisciplinary examination, where experiences from science illuminate endlessly designing developments rouse further organic investigation.

Looking forward, biomimetic paws are ready to assume an undeniably huge part in tending to complex difficulties across different spaces. The joining of these bio-propelled plans into regular advancements can possibly upset businesses, work on clinical intercessions, and add to the improvement of additional reasonable and productive arrangements. As the field keeps on advancing, scientists and designers will probably uncover new features of paw functionalities in nature, prompting developments that push the limits of what is as of now feasible.

The investigation of biomimetic hooks addresses a dazzling excursion into the convergence of science and innovation. From delicate mechanical technology to clinical instruments, materials science, and space investigation, the uses of paw propelled plans grandstand the flexibility and versatility of bio-roused innovations.

As humankind keeps on drawing motivation from the regular world, what's in store holds the commitment of perpetually refined biomimetic paws that upgrade our capacities, work on how we might interpret our general surroundings, and add to a more supportable and agreeable conjunction with the complex plans culminated by development north of millions of years.

Chapter 7

Conservation Challenges

Preservation, in spite of its honorable objectives, faces a variety of perplexing difficulties in the advanced period. As the world wrestles with raising dangers to biodiversity, environments, and the fragile equilibrium of the planet's regular assets, the preservation local area should stand up to diverse snags that request creative arrangements. Understanding these difficulties is pivotal for creating powerful systems that can guarantee the protection of Earth's different environments and the heap species that possess them.

One of the chief difficulties in preservation is environment misfortune and discontinuity, driven fundamentally by human exercises like deforestation, urbanization, and horticultural development. As human populaces thrive and social orders look to satisfy developing needs for assets, immense wraps of regular natural surroundings are being changed over into agrarian fields, framework, and metropolitan regions. This infringement disturbs biological systems, dislodges untamed life, and lessens the accessibility of reasonable natural surroundings for innumerable species.

Living space fracture intensifies the issue, segregating populaces and hindering the normal progression of hereditary variety, prompting expanded weakness to ecological changes and undermining the endurance of various species.

Environmental change remains as really difficult for preservation endeavors. The World's environment is going through remarkable adjustments because of human-incited exercises, principally the arrival of ozone depleting substances into the air. Climbing temperatures, changes in precipitation designs, and the expanded recurrence of outrageous climate occasions present extreme dangers to environments and species around the world. For some organic entities, particularly those with explicit environment necessities, the speed and size of environmental change might exceed their capacity to adjust or move. This can result in bungles among species and their surroundings, disturbing environmental connections, and pushing weak species nearer to termination.

Intrusive species address one more imposing test to preservation. Human exercises, like global exchange and travel, have worked with the accidental acquaintance of non-local species with new areas. These obtrusive species frequently outcompete or go after local verdure, prompting disturbances in biological systems. The deficiency of local biodiversity, modified environmental elements, and the potential for the spread of illnesses can result from obtrusive species, representing a critical danger to the security and flexibility of biological systems.

Overexploitation of regular assets, driven by impractical collecting and fishing rehearses, is a basic test influencing various species and environments. Whether it is overfishing in marine conditions, poaching of untamed life for the unlawful exchange, or logging that surpasses the regenerative limit of woodlands, the steady abuse of normal assets presents serious outcomes. The consumption of fish stocks, the decay of notable species because of poaching, and the deficiency of basic territories highlight the critical requirement for supportable administration practices to offset human necessities with the protection of biological systems.

Contamination, in different structures, presents an unavoidable and slippery danger to biodiversity. From plastic contamination in seas to compound pollutants in freshwater living spaces, contamination can negatively affect the strength of environments and the species they support. Rural spillover, modern releases, and ill-advised garbage removal add to the debasement of water quality, influencing oceanic organic entities and disturbing whole food networks. Air contamination, including poisons that add to corrosive downpour, can have flowing consequences for earthly environments, influencing plant wellbeing and the creatures that rely upon them.

Human-natural life struggle is an undeniably pervasive protection challenge, especially in locales where human populaces infringe upon untamed life environments. Rivalry for assets, like food and water, can prompt struggles among people and untamed life.

Huge carnivores, similar to lions and tigers, may present dangers to domesticated animals, inciting retaliatory killings by networks looking to safeguard their livelihoods. Tending to human-untamed life struggle requires a sensitive harmony between protecting human interests and safeguarding the natural jobs of untamed life, frequently requiring local area commitment, schooling, and the improvement of supportable conjunction methodologies.

The worldwide interconnectedness of environments requires global coordinated effort for compelling preservation. Be that as it may, international difficulties and differences in political will, assets, and limits among countries can obstruct composed endeavors. Transboundary preservation issues, like transitory species that navigate various nations or the administration of shared environments, require global participation and strategy. Connecting these holes and encouraging a common obligation to preservation objectives are fundamental for tending to worldwide ecological difficulties.

The deficiency of biodiversity is a characterizing part of the ongoing time, set apart by a fast decrease in the overflow and assortment of life on The planet. The speed increase of species eradications, frequently credited to human exercises, raises alerts about the disentangling of perplexing environmental organizations. The deficiency of biodiversity not just lessens the inborn worth of different living things yet additionally debilitates the flexibility of biological systems to natural changes. Preservation endeavors are entrusted with the overwhelming test of moderating the continuous biodiversity emergency and forestalling the permanent loss of species and environments.

Asset imperatives and financing limits present significant boundaries to successful preservation activities. As the interest for protection drives increments, insufficient monetary assets can hinder the execution of exhaustive systems. Preservation associations, administrative organizations, and specialists frequently face difficulties in getting financing for research, natural surroundings reclamation, and local area commitment programs. Guaranteeing supported monetary help for preservation exercises is essential for the drawn out progress of drives pointed toward safeguarding biodiversity.

The distinction between protection science and public mindfulness addresses a critical test in gathering support for preservation endeavors. Successful protection requires sound logical exploration as well as open figuring out, commitment, and promotion. Imparting the significance of biodiversity, the effects of human exercises on biological systems, and the advantages of protection measures is fundamental for building a wide body electorate for ecological stewardship. Overcoming any barrier between logical discoveries and public discernment stays a determined test in the preservation scene.

The intricacies of preservation challenges require versatile and interdisciplinary methodologies. Moderates frequently need to explore different social, social, and monetary settings to execute successful methodologies.

At times, protection endeavors might be upset by an absence of nearby local area contribution, lacking thought of customary information, or the burden of hierarchical methodologies that don't line up with the requirements and goals of neighborhood populaces. Embracing a comprehensive and comprehensive methodology that includes networks, regards social qualities, and incorporates conventional natural information is indispensable for accomplishing feasible protection results.

Innovative headways, when applied prudently, can improve preservation endeavors. In any case, the fast speed of mechanical change additionally presents difficulties. The abuse of innovation, for example, the sending of robots or sensors for criminal operations like poaching, highlights the double edged nature of mechanical intercessions. Moral contemplations, security concerns, and the requirement for mindful advancement should direct the mix of innovation into protection techniques.

Preservation challenges are unpredictably connected to more extensive cultural issues, including destitution, imbalance, and impractical utilization designs. As human populaces keep on developing, the interest for assets puts expanding strain on biological systems. Tending to protection challenges requires natural arrangements as well as a thought of the social and financial elements that drive ecological corruption. Maintainable improvement rehearses that focus on ecological preservation close by human prosperity are fundamental for accomplishing an amicable harmony among society and the regular world.

The mind boggling and interconnected nature of preservation challenges requests a thorough and cooperative methodology. The direness of tending to living space misfortune, environmental change, intrusive species, overexploitation, contamination, and different dangers to biodiversity requires purposeful endeavors at nearby, public, and worldwide levels. Protection methodologies should be versatile, interdisciplinary, and comprehensive, incorporating biological, social, and financial contemplations. As mankind wrestles with the significant outcomes of its effect in the world, a promise to preservation isn't just a moral goal yet in addition an essential interest in the drawn out wellbeing and supportability of Earth's environments and the heap species that call it home.

7.1: Threats to Species with Enormous Talons

Species outfitted with tremendous claws, whether flying predators, reptiles, or warm blooded creatures, face a heap of dangers in the cutting edge world. These notorious highlights, advanced over centuries for endurance and predation, presently open these animals to anthropogenic difficulties that endanger their reality. Understanding the dangers to species with gigantic claws is essential for creating preservation techniques that address the complicated interchange between regular variations and the effects of human exercises.

One of the essential dangers to claw bearing species is natural surroundings misfortune and corruption. As human populaces grow and change scenes for agribusiness, metropolitan turn of events, and framework, the regular environments of these species are progressively infringed upon. Flying predators, like birds and falcons, frequently require enormous regions for hunting and settling. Deforestation, transformation of land for agribusiness, and never-ending suburbia reduce the accessibility of appropriate natural surroundings, dividing environments and upsetting the biological equilibrium fundamental for the endurance of claw prepared species.

Environmental change, driven by human-instigated exercises like the consuming of petroleum products, represents a huge danger to animal categories with colossal claws. These animals, finely tuned to explicit ecological circumstances, face difficulties as environment designs shift. Changes in temperature, precipitation, and the recurrence of outrageous climate occasions can affect the accessibility of prey, adjust movement designs, and disturb rearing cycles. Species adjusted to specific climatic zones might find themselves unfit to adapt to quick and unusual changes, expanding the gamble of populace decline and neighborhood eliminations.

Obtrusive species address an inescapable danger to claw prepared species and the environments they possess. The presentation of non-local species, whether purposeful or incidental, can have destroying outcomes. Obtrusive hunters, contenders, or microbes can outcompete local species, prompting decreases in prey populaces or the acquaintance of illnesses with which nearby species might need resistance. For flying predators, this danger is especially intense as obtrusive species may straightforwardly vie for prey or target weak little birds, compounding populace declines.

Human-untamed life struggle represents a critical gamble to animal categories with huge claws, particularly those that come into closeness to human settlements. Flying predators might go after animals, prompting retaliatory killings by ranchers looking to safeguard their livelihoods. This contention can bring about the mistreatment of claw prepared species, with people being intentionally hurt or killed. The deficiency of people, particularly rearing matches, can significantly affect populace elements and ruin protection endeavors.

Overexploitation, driven by unlawful hunting and the untamed life exchange, addresses an immediate danger to animal varieties with significant claws. Raptors, specifically, might be focused on for their claws, feathers, or other body parts, driven by social practices, conventional medication, or the interest for outlandish pets. The overharvesting of people can prompt populace declines, upset social designs, and compromise the hereditary variety fundamental for the drawn out endurance of these species.

Contamination, including synthetic foreign substances, plastic waste, and different poisons, represents a danger to claw prepared species and their living spaces. Flying predators, which possess high trophic levels, may amass poisons through the established pecking order, prompting unfriendly consequences for their wellbeing and conceptive achievement.

Pollutants in water bodies can affect the accessibility of prey, further compromising the feasibility of claw prepared species. Plastic contamination, specifically, represents an immediate danger as these species might ingest or become ensnared in plastic flotsam and jetsam, bringing about injury or passing.

Territory discontinuity, frequently a result of human exercises, can upset the regular ways of behaving and developments of species with colossal claws. Raptors, known for their far reaching regions, may find their searching and settling regions disengaged or decreased in size. Divided environments obstruct the capacity of these species to track down mates, access assets, and keep up with solid populaces. The hereditary disengagement coming about because of living space fracture can prompt diminished hereditary variety, making species more defenseless against sicknesses and natural changes.

Anthropogenic aggravations, like clamor contamination and human exercises in basic environments, can upset claw prepared species, influencing their way of behaving and rearing achievement. Settling locales of flying predators, for instance, might be upset by human exercises, prompting home surrender or decreased regenerative achievement. The responsiveness of these species to aggravations highlights the significance of saving undisturbed territories and limiting human effects in regions urgent for their endurance.

The deficiency of customary prey because of elements like overfishing or environment corruption can represent an immediate danger to animal varieties with tremendous claws, particularly those dependent on unambiguous prey species. For example, falcons might confront provokes in the event that fish populaces decline due to overfishing or ecological changes. The flowing impacts of prey consumption can prompt food deficiencies, lack of healthy sustenance, and populace declines among claw prepared species.

Worldwide peculiarities, for example, the unlawful natural life exchange present extreme dangers to species with important claws. The interest for claws, feathers, or other body parts in conventional medication, elaborate use, or as fascinating pets drives unlawful exchange organizations. This unlawful business can have obliterating ramifications for claw prepared species, as people are caught, moved, and exchanged, frequently prompting high death rates and populace declines. Protection endeavors should not just location the immediate dangers to these species yet in addition battle the basic drivers of the unlawful natural life exchange.

The interconnectedness of biological systems and species implies that the deficiency of claw prepared hunters can have flowing impacts on whole food networks. These species, frequently possessing dominant hunter jobs, assume critical parts in managing prey populaces and keeping up with the natural equilibrium. The downfall or loss of claw prepared species can prompt uncontrolled populace development in prey species, influencing vegetation, and possibly setting off a trophic fountain that resounds all through the biological system.

Protection challenges are additionally exacerbated by restricted assets and contending needs. Protection associations and legislative organizations might confront requirements with regards to financing, faculty, and innovative limit. Adjusting the necessities of species with huge claws against other protection needs, financial contemplations, and social requests requires vital and asset productive methodologies.

Powerful protection techniques for species with gigantic claws should be complete and address both the immediate dangers to these species and the basic drivers of those dangers. Living space assurance and rebuilding, including the making of untamed life passageways to relieve the impacts of fracture, are crucial for guaranteeing the drawn out suitability of these species. Land-use arranging that considers the requirements of claw prepared species and offsets human exercises with protection objectives is fundamental.

Environmental change relief and transformation procedures are pivotal for defending species with tremendous claws notwithstanding an evolving environment. This might include the production of environment strong living spaces, working with species development to follow moving environments, and tending to the more extensive effects of environmental change on prey accessibility and biological system elements.

Obtrusive species the board is a vital part of preservation endeavors, requiring the improvement of strong biosecurity measures to forestall the presentation of intrusive species and the execution of control projects to oversee existing intrusions. Public mindfulness and training efforts assume a fundamental part in forestalling the unexpected presentation of obtrusive species and earning support for protection endeavors.

Supportable advancement rehearses that focus on the protection of normal natural surroundings while addressing the necessities of neighborhood networks are fundamental for tending to human-untamed life struggle. Executing measures to safeguard animals, drawing in with nearby networks in protection navigation, and encouraging conjunction methodologies add to decreasing clash and advancing agreeable cooperations among people and claw prepared species.

The guideline of overexploitation through the implementation of natural life security regulations and the advancement of manageable gathering rehearses is principal. Combatting unlawful untamed life exchange requires global cooperation, policing, and endeavors to address the interest for natural life items. Public mindfulness missions can assume a significant part in lessening the interest for claws and other body parts, in this way checking the unlawful exchange.

Contamination alleviation techniques include the guideline of synthetic impurities, squander the executives to decrease plastic contamination, and endeavors to limit poisons in water bodies.

The improvement of advances and practices that decrease the ecological effect of human exercises, for example, supportable agribusiness and waste decrease measures, adds to limiting contamination dangers to claw prepared species.

Protection drives should likewise zero in on saving conventional prey populaces and addressing difficulties connected with overfishing, natural surroundings debasement, and prey exhaustion. Reasonable fisheries the board, territory rebuilding, and biological system based approaches are indispensable for keeping up with the prey base fundamental for the endurance of claw prepared hunters.

Worldwide participation and backing are basic for tending to worldwide dangers, for example, the unlawful natural life exchange and environmental change. Cooperative endeavors between countries, non-administrative associations, and established researchers can intensify protection influence and work with the sharing of information, assets, and best practices.

Schooling and mindfulness programs assume a crucial part in gathering public help for protection drives. Interfacing individuals with the charming species having colossal claws, featuring their environmental significance, and cultivating a feeling of obligation for their preservation add to building a body electorate for safeguarding these species and their living spaces.

Research is central for grasping the biological prerequisites, ways of behaving, and populace elements of species with gigantic claws. Long haul observing projects, populace appraisals, and logical investigations contribute important information that illuminate protection methodologies and versatile administration draws near.

Species with gigantic claws, encapsulating nature's ability in predation and variation, stand up to a huge number of dangers in the Anthropocene. As humankind wrestles with its effect on the regular world, the protection of these notorious species requires a comprehensive and interdisciplinary methodology. Adjusting the necessities of claw outfitted species with the prerequisites of human social orders, tending to basic drivers of dangers, and cultivating a worldwide obligation to preservation are central. Through coordinated and versatile endeavors, humankind can try to coincide with these grand animals, protecting the natural respectability and biodiversity that characterizes our common planet.

7.2: Habitat Destruction and Climate Change

Territory obliteration and environmental change stand as two interconnected and unavoidable difficulties that have significant ramifications for the strength of our planet's biological systems and the horde species that possess them. The many-sided snare of life on Earth depends vigorously on the honesty and strength of regular natural surroundings, which, thus, are complicatedly connected to the more extensive climatic circumstances that characterize every locale.

Understanding the unique exchange between natural surroundings obliteration and environmental change is fundamental for figuring out viable protection methodologies and addressing the dire need to safeguard biodiversity and relieve the effects of ecological debasement.

Living space Obliteration: A Forerunner to Biodiversity Misfortune

Natural surroundings obliteration, energized by human exercises like deforestation, urbanization, and agrarian extension, stays one of the main dangers to worldwide biodiversity. The change of regular scenes into croplands, logging destinations, or metropolitan regions frequently prompts the discontinuity, corruption, or inside and out loss of basic living spaces for endless species. This tireless change of biological systems disturbs the sensitive equilibrium that has developed over centuries, risking the endurance of various plants, creatures, and microorganisms.

Backwoods, specifically, represent the extensive outcomes of natural surroundings annihilation. Deforestation, driven by the interest for lumber, horticultural land, and different assets, not just lessens the biodiversity of these complicated biological systems yet additionally contributes altogether to environmental change. Woods go about as carbon sinks, retaining significant measures of carbon dioxide (CO_2) from the environment. At the point when trees are felled or consumed, this put away carbon is delivered, worsening the nursery impact and heightening an Earth-wide temperature boost.

Sea-going natural surroundings, including wetlands, coral reefs, and freshwater biological systems, are similarly defenseless against environment obliteration. Metropolitan development, contamination, and unreasonable fishing rehearses put gigantic strain on these biological systems, prompting the downfall of sea-going biodiversity. Coral reefs, frequently alluded to as the rainforests of the ocean, face up and coming dangers from increasing temperatures, contamination, and damaging fishing strategies, all of which add to natural surroundings corruption and the deficiency of marine species.

The results of territory annihilation reach out past the prompt loss of widely varied vegetation. The multifaceted connections between species, finely tuned to explicit biological specialties, are upset. Uprooted or divided populaces face difficulties in tracking down appropriate territories, getting to assets, and keeping up with hereditary variety. The downfall of pollinators, fundamental for the propagation of many plants, and the deficiency of cornerstone species, which assume lopsidedly huge parts in biological systems, highlight the colossal effects of natural surroundings annihilation on biodiversity.

Environmental Change: A Worldwide Test with Expansive Results

Environmental change, driven transcendently by human exercises like the consuming of non-renewable energy sources, deforestation, and modern cycles, addresses a worldwide test with significant ramifications for the planet's biological systems.

The World's environment is going through quick and uncommon changes, appearing in climbing temperatures, adjusted precipitation designs, and an expansion in the recurrence and force of outrageous climate occasions. These progressions resound across environments, influencing species conveyance, movement designs, and the planning of key organic occasions.

One of the most prominent effects of environmental change is the peculiarity of reach shifts, where species push toward higher scopes or heights because of changing temperature systems. This relocation, while permitting a few animal types to follow their favored environment zones, can prompt the fracture of populaces and biological systems. Species adjusted to explicit temperature and precipitation reaches might end up external their ideal circumstances, confronting difficulties in tracking down appropriate natural surroundings and getting to important assets.

The warming of the planet's seas presents huge dangers to marine biological systems. Coral dying, a peculiarity where corals remove the harmonious green growth that furnish them with energy, is connected to raised ocean temperatures. As seas ingest abundance heat from the environment, the fragile equilibrium that supports coral reefs is upset, prompting inescapable blanching occasions and the resulting debasement of these biodiverse biological systems. Furthermore, sea fermentation, a consequence of expanded CO_2 retention, presents endangers to marine life, especially creatures that depend on calcium carbonate for their skeletons and shells.

Changes in precipitation designs add to adjusted water accessibility in different areas, affecting earthbound environments and freshwater natural surroundings. Dry spells and changes in precipitation power can prompt water shortage, influencing both plant and creature species. Wetlands, significant for supporting different natural life and giving fundamental environment administrations, are especially helpless against changes in water accessibility, with ramifications for transient birds, creatures of land and water, and various different species that rely upon these territories.

Outrageous climate occasions, like tropical storms, fierce blazes, and heatwaves, are turning out to be more incessant and serious because of environmental change. These occasions can devastatingly affect biological systems, causing territory obliteration, the deficiency of vegetation, and interruptions to natural cycles. The 2019-2020 Australian bushfires, for instance, featured the devastating results of delayed and extreme out of control fire occasions on famous species like koalas and the interesting biological systems of the landmass.

Interconnected Dangers: Intensifying the Effect on Biodiversity

The basic connection between territory annihilation and environmental change enhances the difficulties looked by biodiversity. In addition to the fact that these peculiarities separately add to the deficiency of species and environments, however they likewise connect in manners that worsen their aggregate effect.

Environment annihilation, by lessening the accessibility of appropriate and interconnected territories, limits the capacity of species to relocate or adjust to changing climatic circumstances. On the other hand, environmental change, by adjusting temperature and precipitation designs, can deliver already appropriate natural surroundings cold, prompting the constriction or loss of biological systems.

The cooperative energy between territory obliteration and environmental change is clear in precipitous areas, where climbing temperatures drive species upslope to look for cooler environments. As they climb, these species frequently experience divided and waning natural surroundings because of deforestation and land-use changes. The outcome is an intensifying impact that confines the accessible space for species to possess, pushing them toward higher heights where reasonable territories might be scant. Snow capped biological systems, portrayed by one of a kind widely varied vegetation adjusted to cold and cruel circumstances, face the inescapable danger of natural surroundings misfortune and discontinuity because of the double tensions of environmental change and human exercises.

Waterfront biological systems, including mangroves, salt bogs, and seagrass beds, additionally defy the double difficulties of natural surroundings obliteration and environmental change. Rising ocean levels, a result of an Earth-wide temperature boost, lead to the immersion of beach front environments, decreasing the accessible space for species that depend on these biological systems. Human exercises, like metropolitan turn of events and hydroponics, further add to the corruption of beach front environments. The mind boggling balance that supports beach front biodiversity is hence disturbed, with expansive ramifications for the heap species that rely upon these momentary zones among land and ocean.

The effects of natural surroundings annihilation and environmental change are eminently articulated in the Cold, where climbing temperatures bring about the liquefying of ocean ice and modifications to earthbound territories. Famous species like polar bears, adjusted to the frosty scenes of the Cold, face living space misfortune as their hunting grounds recoil. Also, the launch of new delivery courses and asset extraction exercises further mixtures the difficulties looked by Icy biological systems, fueling the dangers to biodiversity in this delicate and quickly evolving climate.

Tropical rainforests, frequently alluded to as the lungs of the Earth, typify the complicated transaction between environment obliteration and environmental change. Deforestation, driven by logging, horticulture, and land change, not just decreases the biodiversity of these rich biological systems yet additionally adds to the arrival of put away carbon, enhancing an Earth-wide temperature boost. The deficiency of species in tropical rainforests, a considerable lot of which are yet to be found and portrayed by science, highlights the direness of addressing both territory obliteration and environmental change to safeguard Earth's most naturally different locales.

Preservation Procedures: Exploring a Perplexing Scene

Tending to the interconnected dangers of environment annihilation and environmental change requires diverse and incorporated preservation techniques. Perceiving the collaborations between these difficulties is fundamental for creating arrangements that actually relieve their consolidated effect on biodiversity and environments.

Territory Insurance and Reclamation:

Executing and extending safeguarded regions to shield basic living spaces.

Upholding guidelines to forestall unlawful logging, land clearing, and living space obliteration.

Starting natural surroundings rebuilding activities to restore corrupted environments and reconnect divided scenes.

Environmental Change Relief:

Lessening ozone harming substance discharges through the change to environmentally friendly power sources.

Advancing reasonable land-use practices to sequester carbon and upgrade environment flexibility.

Pushing for worldwide participation and arrangements to address the worldwide test of environmental change.

Feasible Improvement Practices:

Coordinating protection contemplations into metropolitan preparation and foundation advancement.

Advancing feasible farming that offsets human necessities with biological uprightness.

Supporting people group based protection drives that line up with neighborhood livelihoods.

Species-explicit Protection:

Directing examination to comprehend the particular effects of environment annihilation and environmental change on individual species.

Executing designated protection programs for species defenseless against the two dangers.

Using hostage reproducing and renewed introduction projects to support populaces confronting unavoidable decay.

Biological system based Approaches:

Embracing all encompassing methodologies that consider whole biological systems as opposed to detached species.

Cultivating scene scale preservation drives that address territory availability and versatility.

Integrating biological reclamation into environmental change variation methodologies.

Public Mindfulness and Training:

Bringing issues to light about the interconnected idea of environment obliteration and environmental change.

Teaching people in general about the significance of biodiversity and the job of biological systems in environment guideline.

Connecting with networks in protection endeavors to cultivate a feeling of stewardship and obligation.

Worldwide Cooperation:

Working with cooperation between countries to address transboundary challenges presented by natural surroundings obliteration and environmental change.

Supporting worldwide drives and arrangements pointed toward saving biodiversity and moderating environmental change.

Sharing logical information and best practices to upgrade preservation results on a worldwide scale.

Versatile Administration:

Carrying out versatile administration procedures that think about the dynamic and developing nature of biological systems.

Persistently observing and reconsidering protection mediations because of changing ecological circumstances.

Consolidating criticism from neighborhood networks and partners to upgrade the viability of protection drives.

Examination and Advancement:

Putting resources into logical exploration to upgrade comprehension of the effects of environment obliteration and environmental change.

Investigating inventive innovations and approaches for living space rebuilding, environmental change relief, and preservation observing.

Empowering interdisciplinary examination that overcomes any issues between biological, climatological, and sociologies.

Strategy Backing:

Supporting for approaches that focus on preservation and maintainable turn of events.

Drawing in with policymakers to coordinate biodiversity protection and environmental change relief into public and global plans.

Teaming up with non-administrative associations, promotion gatherings, and policymakers to shape regulation that tends to interconnected dangers.

7.3: Conservation Success Stories

Preservation examples of overcoming adversity, against a scenery of ecological difficulties and biodiversity misfortune, offer encouraging signs and motivation.

These accounts exhibit the positive effect of devoted protection endeavors, showing that with key mediations, cooperative drives, and local area commitment, switching the downfall of species and ecosystems is conceivable. These examples of overcoming adversity highlight the significance of gaining from past accomplishments and utilizing aggregate endeavors to address the earnest requirement for worldwide protection.

One praiseworthy example of overcoming adversity rotates around the astounding recuperation of the California condor (Gymnogyps californianus), one of the world's most imperiled bird species. During the 1980s, the number of inhabitants in California condors had dwindled to a simple 27 people, essentially because of lead harming from ingesting spent lead ammo, natural surroundings obliteration, and poaching. Confronted with the inevitable danger of elimination, a striking choice was made to start a hostage rearing project. The excess wild condors were caught and set in rearing offices, and a careful arrangement for renewed introduction was gotten under way.

The hostage reproducing program, drove by the U.S. Fish and Natural life Administration and banding together associations, zeroed in on encouraging a self-supporting populace that could flourish in nature. This included tending to the immediate dangers as well as establishing a steady climate helpful for condor recuperation. The renewed introduction endeavors were met with difficulties, including lead harming from ecological sources, territory misfortune, and the requirement for continuous checking.

Throughout the long term, the committed endeavors paid off. The California condor populace has expanded to more than 500 people, with both hostage and wild populaces adding to the species' recuperation. The progress of this drive features the viability of coordinated protection systems, consolidating hostage reproducing, natural surroundings reclamation, and local area commitment. Continuous endeavors underline the significance of tending to tenacious dangers, for example, lead harming, and keeping a careful way to deal with guarantee the drawn out endurance of the California condor.

The account of the Bedouin oryx (Oryx leucoryx) presents another convincing protection achievement. Local to the deserts of the Middle Eastern Landmass, the Bedouin oryx looked close eradication due to overhunting, environment corruption, and rivalry with homegrown domesticated animals. By the mid 1970s, the species was announced terminated in nature. Be that as it may, a hostage reproducing program started by the Phoenix Zoo as a team with the Sultanate of Oman meant to switch this staggering pattern.

The hostage reproducing program, known as Activity Oryx, zeroed in on rearing Bedouin oryx in bondage and once again introducing them into their local environment. The underlying progress of the program prompted the foundation of safeguarded saves in Oman, giving a solid climate to the oryx to flourish. Throughout the next many years, the hostage reared oryx were progressively once again introduced into the wild, and their populaces started to bounce back.

Today, the Bedouin oryx remains as an image of effective protection, with populaces numbering in the large numbers across the Middle Eastern Promontory. The species has been downsized from "Jeopardized" to "Defenseless" on the Global Association for Preservation of Nature (IUCN) Red Rundown, denoting a critical accomplishment in the continuous endeavors to protect this notorious desert species.

The recuperation of the dim wolf (Canis lupus) in Yellowstone Public Park addresses a milestone example of overcoming adversity in the domain of carnivore protection. By the mid-twentieth 100 years, dark wolves had been extirpated from Yellowstone because of hunter control programs. Perceiving the biological significance of wolves in keeping up with environment balance, renewed introduction endeavors were started in 1995.

23 wolves from Canada were once again introduced to Yellowstone, starting discussion and discussion. Be that as it may, throughout the long term, the positive effect of the renewed introduction became clear. The presence of wolves prompted a trophic fountain, impacting the way of behaving of elk and different ungulates. This, thusly, permitted vegetation to recuperate, helping a scope of animal varieties from beavers to larks. The wolves' effect on the environment showed the complex trap of connections inside biological systems and the flowing impacts of hierarchical guideline.

The Yellowstone wolf renewed introduction fills in as a model for the rebuilding of dominant hunters and represents the significant impact these species can have on whole biological systems. The outcome of this drive has provoked more extensive conversations about the significance of enormous carnivores in keeping up with biodiversity and biological system wellbeing.

In the marine domain, the recuperation of humpback whales (Megaptera novaeangliae) stands apart as a demonstration of the viability of worldwide preservation endeavors. Humpback whales, known for their glorious breaking and complex tunes, were seriously drained because of business whaling exercises in the twentieth 100 years. By the 1960s, a few humpback whale populaces were near the very edge of breakdown.

The worldwide local area mobilized to address the predicament of humpback whales, finishing in the 1986 ban on business whaling forced by the Global Whaling Commission (IWC). The ban gave a respite to humpback whales, permitting their populaces to recuperate without the quick danger of hunting. Accordingly, humpback whale numbers have bounced back, and numerous populaces have been delisted or minimized from "Jeopardized" or "Defenseless" on protection status appraisals.

Preservation measures stretched out past hunting guidelines to incorporate endeavors to lessen transport strikes, relieve snare in fishing gear, and safeguard basic territories. The recuperation of humpback whales exhibits the positive effect of global collaboration, lawful systems, and supported protection estimates in shielding marine megafauna.

Endeavors to moderate the brilliant lion tamarin (Leontopithecus rosalia) exhibit the progress of centered protection systems for jeopardized primates. Local to the Atlantic Timberland in Brazil, the brilliant lion tamarin confronted extreme environment misfortune because of urbanization and horticulture. By the 1960s, the species had become fundamentally imperiled, with two or three hundred people staying in divided territories.

Protection associations, zoos, and the Brazilian government teamed up on a multi-layered way to deal with save the brilliant lion tamarin. Hostage rearing projects were laid out to make a repository of hereditary variety and act as a security net for the species. All the while, environment rebuilding drives planned to reconnect divided backwoods fixes and make passageways for the development of tamarin populaces.

Renewed introduction endeavors included delivering hostage reproduced people into reestablished environments, painstakingly observed to guarantee their variation to nature. The progress of these drives prompted an eminent expansion in brilliant lion tamarin populaces, provoking the renaming of the species from "Imperiled" to "Defenseless" on the IUCN Red Rundown.

The brilliant lion tamarin story represents the significance of coordinating hostage reproducing, territory reclamation, and local area association in primate preservation. The commitment of neighborhood networks in the Atlantic Woods assumed a urgent part, stressing the meaning of human-natural life conjunction in accomplishing economical preservation results.

The recuperation of the southern white rhinoceros (Ceratotherium simum) from the edge of termination remains as a victory in rhinoceros preservation. By the late nineteenth hundred years, southern white rhinos had been diminished to a simple modest bunch of people in South Africa, fundamentally because of serious hunting and environment misfortune. Preservation endeavors in the twentieth 100 years, including the foundation of safeguarded regions and rigid enemy of poaching measures, added to the continuous recuperation of the species.

One significant second in the southern white rhino's preservation history was the formation of the Hluhluwe-iMfolozi Park in South Africa. This save assumed a vital part in securing and reproducing the excess white rhinos, turning into a fortification for the animal varieties. Resulting movements of rhinos to other safeguarded regions and confidential holds additionally supported their populaces.

Lately, imaginative preservation draws near, including local area drove protection drives and high level enemy of poaching advances, have added to the supported recuperation of southern white rhinos. While difficulties, for example, poaching persevere, the southern white rhino's populace has bounced back essentially, denoting a momentous accomplishment in enormous well evolved creature preservation.

The examples of overcoming adversity referenced here feature different ways to deal with preservation, underlining the significance of custom-made procedures for every species and environment. Normal topics across these accounts incorporate the urgent job of cooperation among legislatures, non-administrative associations, neighborhood networks, and established researchers. Preservation achievement frequently includes a blend of natural surroundings security, reclamation, hostage reproducing, and maintainable administration works on, mirroring the intricacy of difficulties looked by species near the precarious edge of termination.

These accounts additionally highlight the requirement for supported endeavors past beginning achievement. Protection is a continuous cycle that requires versatility, cautiousness, and a guarantee to tending to arising dangers. The preservation scene is dynamic, with new difficulties, for example, environmental change, natural surroundings fracture, and arising illnesses requiring imaginative and cooperative arrangements.

The illustrations gained from these examples of overcoming adversity can act as an aide for future protection tries. They stress the significance of drawing in nearby networks as stewards of biodiversity, coordinating logical examination into preservation navigation, and upholding serious areas of strength for structures that safeguard imperiled species and their living spaces. Moreover, these examples of overcoming adversity rouse trust and show that, with deliberate exertion, it is feasible to invert the direction of species decline and reestablish environments to a condition of wellbeing and strength.

Nonetheless, it is pivotal to perceive that not all species have examples of overcoming adversity, and many keep on confronting approaching dangers to their endurance. The continuous loss of biodiversity internationally highlights the desperation of increasing protection endeavors and tending to underlying drivers, for example, natural surroundings obliteration, environmental change, and unreasonable asset double-dealing.

Protection examples of overcoming adversity act as encouraging signs notwithstanding uncommon biodiversity misfortune. They show the way that coordinated and vital endeavors can prompt the recuperation of species, the reclamation of environments, and the safeguarding of our planet's regular legacy. As the worldwide local area faces heightening natural difficulties, these examples of overcoming adversity offer significant experiences and motivation for molding a maintainable and amicable future where people coincide with the rich embroidery of life on The planet.

7.4: Future Prospects for Clawed Creatures

What's in store possibilities for tore animals envelop a perplexing and dynamic scene molded by a conversion of natural, ecological, and anthropogenic variables. As we peer into the distance, it is basic to consider the difficulties and valuable open doors that lie ahead for these interesting and frequently impressive occupants of nature. The direction of mauled animals, going from dominant hunters with imposing claws to more modest species with specific transformations, is complicatedly connected to the more extensive setting of biodiversity protection, environment conservation, and the advancing elements of human-natural life associations.

Natural Versatility and Versatile Limits:

The capacity of ripped at animals to explore changing natural circumstances and human-incited pressures depends on their environmental flexibility and versatile limits. Environmental change, territory fracture, and modifications in prey accessibility present impressive difficulties. Be that as it may, species blessed with flexible ways of behaving, expansive environmental specialties, and hereditary variety might show a more prominent ability to adjust to novel conditions.

Dominant hunters, like huge felines and raptors, frequently have a level of natural versatility that empowers them to take advantage of different living spaces and prey species. Their outcome notwithstanding ecological changes might rely upon the protection of extensive, interconnected scenes that consider regular developments, relocation, and transformation. For more modest species with particular paw variations, for example, arboreal warm blooded creatures and insectivores, the vital lies in protecting their particular living spaces and the environmental connections that support their one of a kind ways of life.

Effect of Natural surroundings Conservation:

The future prosperity of mauled animals is complicatedly attached to the protection of their regular natural surroundings. As human populaces extend, land-use changes and living space annihilation raise, putting gigantic tension on environments. Preservation endeavors should focus on the foundation and support of safeguarded regions, untamed life passages, and cradle zones that empower the free development of species.

The progress of environment conservation lies in the amount of safeguarded land as well as in its quality. Sound environments with different vegetation, reasonable prey populaces, and insignificant human aggravation are fundamental for the supported endurance of pawed animals. The foundation of protection easements and organizations with nearby networks can cultivate concurrence, guaranteeing that both natural life and human necessities are met.

For species with huge claws, for example, hawks and enormous carnivores, broad regions are basic for getting adequate prey and keeping up with solid populaces.

Protection methodologies should be custom-made to address the particular spatial prerequisites of these species, consolidating satellite telemetry and GPS following to comprehend their development examples and territory usage. Moreover, cooperative endeavors between protection associations, states, and nearby networks are fundamental for the compelling execution of living space safeguarding drives.

Human-Natural life Struggle and Moderation:

As human populaces grow and infringe upon natural life living spaces, occasions of human-natural life struggle become more pervasive. Ripped at animals, particularly those with an apparent danger to animals or yields, may confront reprisal from networks looking to safeguard their occupations. Tending to human-natural life struggle requires a diverse methodology that joins local area commitment, schooling, and the improvement of supportable practices.

In locales where huge carnivores, like lions and tigers, exist together with human populaces, carrying out successful struggle moderation measures is essential. This incorporates the utilization of non-deadly hindrances, like secure animals nooks and early-cautioning frameworks, to limit experiences among hunters and homegrown creatures. Besides, people group based protection drives that underscore the concurrence of people and mauled animals can encourage a feeling of shared liability regarding the prosperity of both.

For species with specific hooks utilized in searching or guard, for example, insect eating animals and pangolins, human-natural life struggle might emerge from errors or unplanned experiences. Training efforts pointed toward bringing issues to light about the biological significance of these species and advancing tranquil conjunction can add to lessening struggle and encouraging an uplifting outlook towards the protection of mauled animals.

Mechanical Advances in Protection:

The fate of pawed animals is personally connected to mechanical developments that improve how we might interpret their way of behaving, biology, and protection needs. The utilization of cutting edge GPS beacons, camera traps, and remote detecting advances has upset natural life observing and research. For species with slippery ways of behaving or those occupying remote and testing landscapes, these innovative devices give remarkable experiences into their lives.

Satellite telemetry permits researchers to follow the developments of huge hunters, screen transient examples, and distinguish basic natural surroundings. This data is significant for illuminating preservation systems, outlining safeguarded regions, and tending to likely dangers. Moreover, the utilization of camera traps empowers specialists to notice subtle species without direct human obstruction, giving a non-meddlesome method for concentrating on their ways of behaving and populace elements.

Headways in hereditary examination and DNA sequencing offer a useful asset for grasping the hereditary variety, relatedness, and wellbeing of torn animal populaces. This data is instrumental for planning successful protection rearing projects, recognizing people for renewed introduction endeavors, and surveying the in general hereditary feasibility of populaces.

Robots and flying reviews add to territory checking and appraisal, especially in extensive scenes. This innovation supports distinguishing changes in land cover, planning territory discontinuity, and looking over natural life populaces. By joining these innovative progressions, traditionalists can foster proof based techniques to protect the fate of ripped at animals.

Preservation Past Boundaries:

The preservation of pawed animals frequently rises above public lines, requiring global participation and cooperative endeavors. Numerous species with broad reaches, like transient birds and huge vertebrates, navigate various nations during their yearly cycles. Safeguarding these species requires facilitated preservation systems that include adjoining countries, shared research drives, and the foundation of transboundary safeguarded regions.

Transient birds, described by their claws adjusted for holding branches or prey, face dangers along their whole flyways. Joint effort between nations along these flyways is basic for guaranteeing the protection of rearing, visit, and wintering environments. Peaceful accords, like the Ramsar Show on Wetlands and the Show on Transient Species, give systems to cooperative protection endeavors on a worldwide scale.

For dominant hunters like the Siberian tiger and the Andean condor, which cross tremendous domains, worldwide joint effort is key. The foundation of transboundary safeguarded regions, joint exploration drives, and the sharing of protection best practices add to the conservation of these notable species. Moreover, drives that include nearby networks on the two sides of lines cultivate a feeling of shared liability regarding the preservation of torn animals.

Environmental Change and Transformation Methodologies:

Environmental change represents a huge and heightening danger to the fate of ripped at animals. Changes in temperature, precipitation designs, and the recurrence of outrageous climate occasions can affect the dispersion, overflow, and conduct of species. Preservation systems should consolidate environment variation measures to guarantee the flexibility of ripped at animals even with an evolving environment.

Species with explicit territory prerequisites, like those ward on high-elevation biological systems or polar locales, may confront the test of natural surroundings misfortune as environment zones shift. Preservation endeavors should zero in on distinguishing appropriate elective territories and making relocation hallways that empower species to move because of changing climatic circumstances.

Conduct variations, like adjustments in scavenging examples or changes in transitory courses, might be seen in light of environment actuated shifts in prey accessibility or vegetation elements. Long haul checking and research are significant for figuring out these transformations and illuminating protection methodologies that record for the unique idea of species' reactions to environmental change.

Besides, integrating environment savvy preservation rehearses, like territory reclamation and the advancement of biological system strength, can improve the capacity of mauled animals to endure the effects of environmental change. Traditionalists should team up with environment researchers to foster prescient models that expect the likely impacts of environmental change on various species and biological systems, taking into account proactive and versatile protection measures.

Social Points of view and Protection Morals:

The protection of mauled animals isn't just a natural objective yet in addition a social and moral obligation. Numerous social orders all over the planet harbor social convictions, fantasies, and customs that include pawed animals, taking into account them as images of solidarity, flexibility, or otherworldly importance. Perceiving and regarding these social points of view is fundamental for cultivating nearby help for protection drives.

Drawing in with neighborhood networks and coordinating customary biological information into protection arranging can prompt more successful and socially touchy methodologies. The consideration of native networks in dynamic cycles guarantees that preservation endeavors line up with nearby qualities and works on, adding to maintainable and local area driven protection results.

Besides, encouraging a protection ethic that rises above social limits is fundamental for ingraining a feeling of worldwide obligation regarding the safeguarding of biodiversity. Training programs, outreach drives, and mindfulness missions can assume a urgent part in advancing preservation morals and moving people to add to the prosperity of ripped at animals and their environments.

Preservation Subsidizing and Monetary Systems:

The monetary help expected for compelling protection measures addresses a basic consider deciding what's in store possibilities of mauled animals. Satisfactory financing is fundamental for living space protection, hostile to poaching endeavors, research drives, and local area commitment programs. The broadening of financing sources, including government portions, altruism, corporate organizations, and worldwide awards, is essential for supporting long haul preservation endeavors.

Creative monetary systems, for example, installments for environment administrations and biodiversity balances, offer promising roads for producing assets for preservation.

These components perceive the characteristic worth of unblemished biological systems and give motivating forces to landowners and networks to effectively take part in protection rehearses. Besides, private-area commitment through corporate social obligation drives and maintainable strategic policies can add to protection financing.

The foundation of preservation gifts and trust reserves guarantees a consistent and solid stream of subsidizing for long haul projects. Cooperative endeavors between legislative organizations, non-benefit associations, and the confidential area can make collaborations that amplify the effect of accessible assets.

Public Mindfulness and Support:

The job of public mindfulness and promotion in forming the fate of mauled animals couldn't possibly be more significant. Educated and connected with networks are bound to help preservation drives, take part in resident science activities, and supporter for strategies that focus on the security of untamed life and their environments.

Training programs focused on at schools, nearby networks, and online stages can bring issues to light about the environmental significance of pawed animals and the dangers they face. Zoos, aquariums, and untamed life safe-havens assume a vital part in teaching general society about the protection needs of mauled animals, encouraging an association among individuals and the normal world.

Backing endeavors pointed toward impacting strategy choices, advancing economical practices, and battling unlawful untamed life exchange add to a favorable climate for preservation. The force of online entertainment and computerized correspondence stages can be bridled to prepare public help, accumulating consideration for basic protection issues and driving aggregate activity.

Moral Untamed life The travel industry:

The eventual fate of pawed animals is inherently connected to the moral elements of untamed life the travel industry. Feasible and dependable untamed life the travel industry can give financial advantages to neighborhood networks, add to preservation subsidizing, and bring issues to light about the benefit of safeguarding normal natural surroundings. Notwithstanding, ineffectively oversaw the travel industry can present huge dangers to untamed life through territory unsettling influence, expanded human-untamed life communications, and the potential for sickness transmission.

Rules for moral untamed life the travel industry ought to focus on the prosperity of pawed animals, stressing negligible effect on their regular ways of behaving and environments. Dependable the travel industry administrators stick to severe sets of rules, guaranteeing that guest exercises don't think twice about government assistance of untamed life. Drives that advance mindful untamed life the travel industry, support nearby networks, and add to preservation endeavors can assume a useful part in store for mauled animals.